Dear Younger Me

Dear Younger Me

WHAT 35
Trailblazing Women
WISH THEY'D KNOWN AS GIRLS

ELISA BOXER

Foreword by **GABBY GIFFORDS**

ROWMAN & LITTLEFIELD
Lanham • Boulder • New York • London

Published by Rowman & Littlefield
An imprint of The Rowman & Littlefield Publishing Group, Inc.
4501 Forbes Boulevard, Suite 200, Lanham, Maryland 20706
www.rowman.com

86-90 Paul Street, London EC2A 4NE, United Kingdom

British Library Cataloguing in Publication Information available

Library of Congress Cataloging-in-Publication Data Available

ISBN 9781538175514 (cloth : alk. paper) | ISBN 9781538175521 (epub)

♾™ The paper used in this publication meets the minimum requirements of
American National Standard for Information Sciences—Permanence of Paper
for Printed Library Materials, ANSI/NISO Z39.48-1992.

Dear Younger Me,
This one's for you.

And for Lisbeth, whose friendship transcends time.

CONTENTS

FOREWORD

Gabby Giffords

WHEN I WAS ELECTED TO THE ARIZONA STATE SENATE IN 2002, I was the youngest woman ever elected to that body. Being a young woman, especially in politics, can be hard. But it's important that our voices are heard. That's why I was honored to participate in this book, along with thirty-four other strong, courageous women, to share advice on what we wished we knew when we were younger and to encourage future generations to speak up and be their best selves.

My life took a much different path than I thought it would after I was shot in the head during a constituent event in 2011. As a result, I now live with aphasia, a communication disorder that sometimes makes speaking hard—but I have not lost my voice.

I've worked hard to regain the ability to walk and talk. Today, I lead GIFFORDS, one of the largest gun violence prevention organizations in the country. In the past ten years, we've taken on the gun lobby to help pass more than 525 gun safety laws in nearly every state, as well as the Bipartisan Safer Communities Act, the first federal gun safety legislation in almost thirty years. Our mission is to stop gun violence and save lives.

When we founded GIFFORDS, people thought our mission was impossible. But we're doing it every day.

I hope as you read the stories of other women in this book, it gives you the determination and inspiration to tackle hard things, be courageous, and be your best. As I like to say, keep moving ahead, and don't look back. You got this!

Love,
Gabby

INTRODUCTION

Books written by the author as a child. PHOTO BY ELISA BOXER

Dear Younger Me,

Keep writing! Your books will one day be on store and library shelves, with bindings a bit more secure than staples.

Those books will feature trailblazing, rabble-rousing women, unafraid to challenge social norms and stand up for what they believe in.

And then, in 2020, when the world is locked down during the COVID pandemic, you will begin reaching out to more of those barrier-breaking women, asking them what they wish their younger selves had known.

Your plan, depending on whether you hear back from any of these women, is to gather their wisdom and write a book.

I'm happy to tell you that the responses will be immediate and overwhelming. Personal heroes of yours will become friends as you correspond with them over the course of creating this book.

You know how you've always been interested in interviewing people around you and writing down what they say? It annoys the heck out of your babysitters when you make them answer your probing questions, but it will lead to a career as a reporter. Some of your most meaningful interviews will be with people who have come through tragedies, reflecting on their lives and realizing what matters.

That yearning to preserve people's stories and legacies will turn personal in your late twenties, when you will receive the news that your beloved Nana Eva doesn't have much longer to live.

Knowing this, please cherish your time with her accordingly.

But also know that years later, many of her most precious qualities will return to you in your son, Evan. Oh my goodness, wait until you meet him.

The year before you get married, you will sit by Nana's bedside, hold her hand, and ask her what she wishes she had known.

Tomorrow will be better, she'll tell you. *Make allowances for the people you love. And for heaven's sake, order the baked stuffed lobster.*

This will ignite a spark. Although you unfortunately develop an allergy to shellfish, the baked stuffed lobster will come to symbolize the importance of allowing yourself to embrace every aspect of this life as fully as you possibly can. It's one of the best pieces of advice you've ever been given, and you'll begin thinking about maybe writing a book someday, with pages filled with wisdom from women you admire.

Here we are.

You were born into a decade when women still weren't allowed to get a credit card or start a business without a male cosigner. Remember that book *Girls Can Be Anything*? It was one of your favorites. Every time Mom and Dad would read it to you, something deep within you stirred with a sense of possibility.

But while that book emphasized the professional potential of women, it featured a young girl having to gather anecdotal evidence and present proof to convince her male kindergarten counterpart that, in fact, girls could be anything.

We've come a long way. But while the pendulum is swinging more toward equal opportunities, recognition, and pay for women, it seems that often the focus is on *doing* rather than *being*: pushing, striving, accomplishing, convincing, rather than emerging as the truest version of who we are and allowing that to speak for itself.

That's one of the main reasons why I found the advice from the women in this book so valuable for young readers.

Essentially, they all offered some version of the fact that by being who we are, authentically and unapologetically, we can accomplish anything. It's an important reminder.

While the women in this book submitted a wide range of responses to what they wish their younger selves had known, the common thread was this: Nothing within us needs to be changed or fixed or improved before we can get out there and share our gifts with the world.

We just have to give ourselves permission to connect with those gifts in the first place, by remembering who we uniquely are.

May this book help our readers remember.

I'll leave you with some advice I wish I had known at your age: Trust your gut. Take your time. Listen to your inner voice above all others. Sit with the underdog. Be gentle with yourself. It's okay to start over. Angels are real. So are miracles. You'll recognize both when they appear. Try to experience awe and wonder at least once a day. Allow periods of rest and stillness. Look up at the sky more. Sometimes fear will show up to keep you safe. Other times it will show up to keep you small. Know the difference. It's okay to change your mind. Do the thing. Never hide any part of who you are. Say the thing. Always have your own back. Be bold in standing up for yourself and those you love. Feel everything, even the hard stuff. Your sensitivity is your superpower. Lead with love.

And please, save those letters from Nana. One day you'll look back and wish you had.

CHAPTER ONE
Manal al-Sharif
WOMEN'S RIGHTS ACTIVIST

Manal al-Sharif. COURTESY OF MANAL AL-SHARIF

Manal al-Sharif made headlines around the world when she got behind the wheel of a car, defying Saudi Arabia's ban on women drivers. She was thrown in jail and released only after signing pledges to never drive again, never speak about driving, and never give any interviews about what she had done.

"They shut you up," she said. "It's disheartening."[1]

But trying to silence a revolutionary tends to backfire.

"When I left jail, do you think I stopped talking? I didn't," she said. "I filed a lawsuit against the traffic police, and I wrote a whole book about it."[2]

That best-selling book, *Daring to Drive: A Saudi Woman's Awakening*, was listed as a #1 summer read by *O, The Oprah Magazine*. The book chronicles Manal's radical Islamic upbringing, her eventual awakening, and her courageous resistance that resulted in international attention and led to Saudi Arabia lifting its ban on women drivers in 2018.

But before that, "I cried on the streets of Saudi Arabia," Manal wrote in a 2017 *Washington Post* opinion piece. "I cried because after a doctor's appointment, I could not find a male driver to take me home. I had to endure harassment as I walked alone. . . . I knew how to drive, but the government would not allow it. To drive while female was punishable by arrest and jail time."[3]

At that time, Saudi women had to either hire private drivers or ask their fathers, husbands, brothers, or sons to drive them wherever they needed to go. Hiring a private driver could cost up to two-thirds of a woman's salary, and as a result, only 15 percent of Saudi women were able to work outside the home.

"In desperation," Manal wrote, "women without access to male drivers have put boys as young as 9 years old behind the wheel, propped up on pillows to see over the dashboard. It is no wonder that the kingdom has among the highest traffic fatality rates in the world."[4]

In 2011, Manal's desire to create change fueled her decision to get behind the wheel. She felt the frustration of having her driver's license but not being allowed to use it. She got in a car, filmed herself driving, and uploaded the video to YouTube and Facebook, where it went viral.

Then the Saudi police threw her in jail. Twice.

When she got out, she became a prominent voice for women's empowerment and gender equality. *Time* magazine named her one of the most influential people in the world. In addition to challenging the female driving ban in Saudi Arabia, Manal has started movements to fight discrimination and abuse, including #IAmLama, which helped create Saudi Arabia's first anti–domestic violence law. She also started #IAmMyOwnGuardian to raise awareness about, and bring an end to, male guardianship laws that require women to get permission of a man to do things like attend classes or go to the hospital. When Manal turned forty, she noted, her son was still her legal guardian.

In drawing attention to the guardianship laws and to the fact that women are jailed in Saudi Arabia for trying to leave their abusive husbands, Manal sees herself as speaking on behalf of those who have been conditioned to stay silent. In doing so, she has built a resilience that supports her in her continued efforts to fight for human rights.

"When you speak up, you're speaking for those . . . who are voiceless," she said, "who are most vulnerable in your societies. And I think that is what builds resilience. Resilience means when you are down, you forgive, you get up, and you continue. For me that is resilience."[5]

With that resilience has come an awareness about the importance of forgiveness.

"In your life there will be things, bad things happen to you, sometimes from the closest people in your life," she said. "I felt like I was betrayed by a whole country, when I just challenged the status quo. I think the most challenging, the most courageous, the most rebellious thing I did in my life wasn't driving a car, or removing my hijab, or speaking against the status quo. It was really forgiving those who did me wrong. And forgiveness is very important because you do it for yourself first. Because it weighs you down, that hate. It weighs you down, that anger. And when you shed that, guess what? You really strip them away from their strongest weapon. It's to intimidate you, to make you afraid."[6]

For Manal, knowing that women all over the world are still being treated as property and being jailed when they fight for their rights fuels her advocacy efforts. And although her most public display of civil disobedience involved getting behind the wheel, she said it was really about so much more than that.

"The key to change in my country for us as women activists was the key to drive our cars," she said. "Because it wasn't about driving a car. It was about driving our own destiny."[7]

Dear Younger Me,

Question the system, never yourself. When it feels wrong, when it makes you feel not worth it, it's because it is wrong, not you. Don't bother so much with people's opinions. When you want to do something, do it because you really want it, but never to prove yourself to others. Nothing will come to you; you need to know what you want and get it. No one will hand you favors; you will have to earn it and work for it. Also, make sure your impactability, not employability, is your goal when you choose a career.

CHAPTER TWO

Dr. Katrin Amunts

NEUROSCIENTIST

Dr. Katrin Amunts. PHOTO BY MAREEN FISCHINGER FOTOGRAFIE, COURTESY OF
DR. KATRIN AMUNTS

KATRIN AMUNTS, PHD, IS WIDELY RECOGNIZED AS ONE OF the world's most prominent neuroscientists. As scientific research director of the Human Brain Project and a professor who directs the Institute for Brain Research at the University of Dusseldorf in Germany, she led a team of researchers developing software to create a 3D map of the human brain— "Google maps of the brain," she called it.[1]

She did it by carefully dissecting donor brains into thousands of slices each, then digitally put them back together in a way that allowed her to research the composition and connections of the brain, right down to the level of each individual nerve fiber.

It is the most detailed model of the brain ever created, and *MIT Technology Review* called it one of the world's most influential technologies. Because of Katrin's work, scientists are now able to study the processes and functions that take place in the brain, helping to improve understanding of neurological disorders like dementia, depression, and Parkinson's disease. Katrin's research is also making it easier for scientists to study the way drugs interact with diseases in the brain, which will eventually lead to specialized medicine and treatments.

Katrin has had a keen interest in science ever since she was a child growing up in communist East Germany. In ninth grade, she moved to a school with a special focus on math and physics. It was there that she was assigned a project that would ignite her lifelong interest in applying physics to hands-on innovations.

"I found it sometimes difficult to understand how precisely physical equations translate into nature and real life," she said. "But then we were given the task of building a resonant circuit consisting of an inductor and a capacitor connected together. That worked nicely, and suddenly we were able to receive a radio station. That awakened my interest in physics."[2]

Interestingly, the radio station the students picked up was one the communist government had forbidden them from accessing.

"The station I received was Rias Berlin, which came from the western part of the city and that was actually not allowed. But what were we supposed to do? It just happened to be the strongest station we heard with our little receiver," she said.[3]

Katrin, who went on to study medicine and biophysics, was always drawn to brain science specifically.

"The human brain has always fascinated me," she said. "It is one of the most complex systems in nature, and we try to identify the principles of its organization. In addition, it changes throughout the whole lifespan and varies between human subjects. To understand what these variations mean, for example with respect to a certain cognitive function or for a disease process, is a highly interesting topic of research."[4]

In addition to being world renowned for her brain mapping, Katrin is also known internationally for breaking gender barriers. She is the only woman among the leaders of the Human Brain Project, and she is routinely touted as one of the most trailblazing women in science.

"I actually grew up taking it for granted that I had the same career opportunities and choices as men," she said in an article showcasing female innovators in medical science. "Only when I entered my first leadership role it became very clear to me that women are underrepresented in these positions and that it is extraordinary to have reached this level. A moment that particularly stuck with me was when I became a full professor as one of only four women in the entire faculty of medicine."[5]

But Katrin also emphasized the importance of institutions hiring women because of their abilities and strengths, not just because of their gender.

7

"I believe it to be crucial that we win over decision-makers to drive gender equality top-down. For real change to happen, decision-makers need to be convinced by the direct benefits of more equality rather than being driven by the desire to act politically correct," she said, adding that equality should be embraced by both men and women together.[6]

"Research on the impact of gender equality on the success of industrial and academic organizations provides very important data to support the argument," she said. "More such studies should be supported. Men and women need to drive equality together; both need to see the advantages, and both will benefit from the changes."[7]

Katrin is active in encouraging more young women to enter science, technology, engineering, and mathematics (STEM) fields, and has this advice for aspiring scientists: "Choose a field in which you are really interested! Intrinsic motivation is absolutely fundamental to pursue a career in science, and also to enjoy it! Strive for realizing your ideas and don't stop just because someone does not like them. Work hard! Build up your own network and consider the support of eminent, senior scientists!"[8]

Dear Younger Me,

When I was your age, I had no doubt that men and women were equal in terms of opportunities, freedom of choice, career prospects, etc. Only later did I learn that this is not always true, although the situation in society in general has changed positively in the meantime. Young women today can find a lot of support to advance their careers, for example. Nevertheless, I think that questions of equality, which are also questions of cultural coexistence, do not always change as quickly as we would like. I therefore think it is important not to give up when you encounter resistance, and not to simply take the achievements of recent years for granted.

CHAPTER THREE
Renae Bluitt
STORYTELLER AND ADVOCATE FOR BLACK WOMEN ENTREPRENEURS

Renae Bluitt. PHOTO BY NIGIL CRAWFORD, COURTESY OF RENAE BLUITT

Black women represent the fastest-growing group of entrepreneurs in America, and Renae Bluitt is making it her business to bring attention to that trend.

Renae is an entrepreneur who has spent her career amplifying the achievements of Black women in business and advocating for the accurate representation of Black women in the media.

In 2020, *Insider* magazine named her as one of the "women whose accomplishments will change the world." Her latest venture is a Netflix documentary called *She Did That*, which showcases the success of Black women–owned businesses. It also highlights the unique challenges and obstacles faced by female founders—obstacles like the funding gap for women of color.

"Black women and the magic we create is the inspiration behind this film," Renae told *Forbes* magazine. "We are literally turning water into wine in spite of the many obstacles we face on our entrepreneurial journeys. . . . This film was created to let the world know what it really takes to be a successful Black woman entrepreneur in this world. Platforms like social media only show us the results and the highlights, but *She Did That* pulls back the curtain to reveal how and why we do it."[1]

The documentary is an outgrowth of Renae's long-running blog *In Her Shoes*, which gives readers an in-depth look at Black women who have overcome significant challenges, such as disproportionately lower funding, to build successful brands. She knew she wanted to expand the conversation to reach a wider audience and include a new medium.

With the documentary, Renae was intentional about hiring Black women for every aspect of production. From the creatives to the makeup artists to the production staff to the people who owned the spaces rented for filming, she wanted to make sure the entire endeavor supported the spirit of Black entrepreneurship. She held screenings across the country, featuring panel discussions full of advice, encouragement, and concrete resources for entrepreneurs looking to expand their businesses.

"I've always been intrigued by other women's stories," Renae said, "their 'ah-ha' moments, successes, struggles, and most importantly, what inspires them to fight the good fight when times get tough."[2]

One woman featured in the film, for example, is a domestic violence survivor who took the trauma of her experience and turned it into a business called My Fab Finance Platform, a collection of online money tools like budget templates and expense trackers. The goal is to empower women so they don't have to stay in unsafe relationships because of financial limitations.

"I want women to know they are not alone in their fears," Renae said. "The biggest takeaway is this—if the women in this film can do it, you can do it, too!"[3]

Renae herself overcame financial and emotional barriers in order to be able to make the film in the first place. After investing as much of her own money as she could in the project and enlisting the help of corporate sponsors, she was disheartened to realize she still didn't have enough to cover the film's budget. But abandoning the project wasn't an option. Even though it has always been a personal challenge for her to ask for help, she knew that in this case she needed to face that fear. She did that by launching a GoFundMe campaign to ask the community for help in bringing her dream to fruition.

"Entrepreneurship can be a lonely journey, particularly for Black women who may not have the resources to hire a team," Renae said. "I want women to know that even the most successful women in business have experienced the challenges and obstacles they face while building their brands. We all make mistakes, learn from them, and stop to refuel or keep going even stronger."[4]

There are nearly two million Black women–owned businesses in the United States, generating more than $51 billion in revenue. Renae wants to boost those numbers even higher by inspiring new changemakers to turn their obstacles into opportunities.

She also wants the next generation of Black leaders to feel a sense of community and confidence, and to know their own personal value. In the spirit of inspiring a new wave of trailblazers, she created an online community where established and aspiring entrepreneurs can connect with one another. Among those aspiring business owners was a group of girls, all under the age of eleven, who opened their own nail salon on their front steps. Renae gave them an award and arranged an internship for them at a nail salon owned by a Black female entrepreneur.

Business runs in Renae's blood. Her grandfather and her father both worked tirelessly on a General Motors assembly line while building their own businesses.

"As a little brown girl growing up in Indiana, I learned so much about the importance of working hard and having a strong work ethic, no matter what position you're in," she said. "These men took pride in their jobs and built their personal brands long before becoming their own bosses. I carry this lesson with me every single day."[5]

In a full-circle development, General Motors became a corporate sponsor for *She Did That*. Renae was thrilled to partner with the company that had employed her father and grandfather in bringing the film to life. She wants her own story, as well as the stories of the women featured in the film, to be a source of inspiration and motivation. But ultimately, she wants women to honor their own unique vision and follow what aligns with them personally.

"The path to personal success looks different for everyone," she said. "Your journey won't look like anyone else's, but the beauty of your story is what makes you, you. It's your special sauce and no one can duplicate that."[6]

Dear Younger Me,

This world will condition you to believe that you need to be something more than who you currently are to be worthy. Please know that love, joy, prosperity, and anything your heart desires is your birthright. You are more than enough and beyond worthy, just the way you are.

CHAPTER FOUR

May Boeve

CLIMATE CHANGE ACTIVIST

May Boeve. COURTESY OF 350.ORG

MAY BOEVE BEGAN HER SOCIAL ACTION EFFORTS AT THE TEN-
der age of four, when she wrote a letter to President George H.
W. Bush asking him to stop cruelty to animals, including bugs.

"I had very supportive parents who encouraged me to
speak up about what I believed in," she said. "So this was the
first of many letter-writing efforts, which went on to holding
lemonade stands and donating the money to charity."[1]

Her social activism grew right along with her. While she
was a student at Middlebury College, she and a small group
of environmentally conscious friends organized a protest at a
nearby mill where tires were being burned. They also launched
a successful campaign to make Middlebury's campus carbon
neutral. And then they joined forces with environmentalist Bill
McKibben, credited with being the first author to raise alarm
bells about the global warming crisis.

The group, just seven people sitting around a folding table,
got in touch with environmental and social justice organizations all over the globe, inviting them to join in a worldwide
day of protesting climate change.

"I believed in the power of collective action and being
part of something bigger than myself," May said. "I knew that
if we were united in our advocacy, that we could make major
change happen."[2]

And they did. In 2009, people in 181 countries came
together for the International Day of Climate Action. CNN
reported that it was "the most widespread day of political
action in our planet's history."[3]

It was the beginning of 350.org, a grassroots nonprofit
that has grown into one of the world's most successful and
disruptive climate change campaigns, with the goal of stopping
all new fossil fuel (coal, oil, gas) projects and transitioning to
renewable energy like solar and wind power.

May is 350.org's executive director. The number 350 refers to the amount of carbon dioxide (350 parts per million) the atmosphere can hold without negatively impacting our climate. But that number has already risen to around 400 parts per million.

Two years after the first International Day of Climate Action, May was handcuffed and arrested outside the White House while protesting the controversial Keystone XL pipeline, designed to transport oil from Canada to the United States. 350.org called it "one of North America's most dangerous pipelines" and was one of the organizations that spearheaded the protest.[4]

"For the months leading up to it, I was very worried about the risks surrounding the entire action," May said. "But as soon as I was there, surrounded by all the other activists, I felt comforted and brave."[5]

After years of legal battles, President Barack Obama rejected the pipeline in 2015.

That same year, *Time* magazine hailed May as a Next Generation Leader, highlighting her ability to bring different groups to the table, build bridges, make compromises, and find common ground to combat the climate crisis.

May told *Time* that climate change really encompasses and connects a wide range of issues: "What I like to do is figure out, based on what another organization does, how does it connect to climate change and how does our work connect to what they do?"[6]

The following year, 350.org launched the #ExxonKnew campaign after finding out that the fossil fuel corporation knew about climate change going back to the 1960s but did nothing to stop it.

A major focus for May and 350.org has been bringing about policy change by pressuring the world's largest institutions to pull their money out of coal, oil, and gas companies. As a result, hundreds of institutions like universities, cities, foundations, and churches have agreed to stop investing in fossil fuels. It's been an "innovative and highly successful" campaign, according to the 2017 announcement from the John F. Kennedy Presidential Library naming May a recipient of the New Frontier Award.[7]

"We have to transform the world, and we can do that through the clean energy transformation that the climate crisis is urging us to do," May said upon receiving the New Frontier Award.[8]

"We can create and transform a world through clean energy that is localized, that creates jobs that are safer for workers, and that helps reconnect people in their communities out of isolation and toward togetherness. It's all very possible," she said. "We have the tools, and we have the movement."[9]

May emphasized the importance of collaboration in achieving 350.org's goals.

"The *we* here is very important," she said. "The *we* is much bigger than 350.org. It's a vast network of individuals, organizations, and movements working together."[10]

Dear Younger Me,

Yes, the world is full of injustices of all kinds. AND the world is full of wonderful people who, like you, want to make it a better place. Surround yourself with them and together you can do great things.

CHAPTER FIVE
Dr. Joan Borysenko
PSYCHONEUROIMMUNOLOGIST

Dr. Joan Borysenko. PHOTO BY ANTON BRKIĆ, COURTESY OF
DR. JOAN BORYSENKO

JOAN BORYSENKO, PHD, IS ONE OF THE WORLD'S LEADING experts on integrative medicine and the mind-body connection. She earned her doctorate in medical sciences from Harvard Medical School, then went on to complete postdoctoral training in cancer cell biology. From there, she became an assistant professor at Tufts Medical School, specializing in cancer research.

And then, she said, "my world shifted on its axis."[1]

Her father was diagnosed with leukemia. He was treated with a medication that drastically altered his mind and behavior, inducing a manic psychosis. He went from being kind and gentle to talking nonstop, being unable to listen, and sometimes becoming combative.

"It was like a stranger had moved into his skin and he had gone missing," Joan recalled. "Our family was in crisis, but the doctor was adamant that he had to take the medication. Quality of life wasn't part of the equation."

One year later, doctors took her father off the medication in preparation for surgery.

"Almost immediately he came back into his right mind," she said. "We were overjoyed. It was as if the survivor of a shipwreck had turned up miraculously on a life raft."

After his surgery, Joan's father was loving, present, and calm—"in retrospect, too calm," she said.

One night, soon after a conversation with Joan, he waited until his wife went to sleep and ended his life by jumping out the window of their high-rise condominium. The family was devastated. Joan saw it as a tragedy that could have been prevented.

"My father didn't die from cancer," she said. "He died from the fact that no one in the hospital had given him or our family any help navigating a devastating medical situation.

My father was more than a disease. He was a human being in deep distress."

Even if her father's cancer couldn't be cured, Joan said, "he and our family might have experienced healing . . . growing together, finding meaning and celebrating his life and legacy. At the very least, we needed some help in coping with the immediate and horrific effects of the treatment."

At the time, Joan was working on government research grants in cancer cell biology. But after she finished those, she refocused her attention "from cancer cells to the person with cancer."

She retrained as a psychologist, "with the hope that if I could help even one family have a better outcome than ours, my father's death might lead to a positive change."

Joan met with renowned doctor Herbert Benson, MD, a cardiologist who was the first person to identify the relaxation response, eventually bringing meditation into mainstream medicine. She had worked with him many years earlier as a research technician during the summer before grad school.

When Joan told Benson about the circumstances leading up to her father's death, he offered her a postdoctorate spot doing research into a then-new field called behavioral medicine. She would be studying the physiology of meditation and the mind-body connection with Benson at Harvard under a grant from the National Institutes of Health.

"Many of my colleagues thought I was nuts," she recalled. But she took him up on his offer. It was a natural fit, given her fascination with the power of the mind to influence the body, which had been percolating since she was a young girl.

Joan recalled one instance from childhood involving her uncle, who was "famous for hating cheese."

One night when he was visiting, Joan's mother baked "a gorgeous cake covered with strawberries and sparkling with an inviting glaze."

Her uncle ate a piece of the cake and loved it so much that he asked for seconds.

He then asked what kind of cake it was.

When her mother told him it was cheesecake, he "pivoted away from the table, gagging, and unceremoniously threw up on the dining room rug."

That event made a monumental impression on young Joan, who realized "it wasn't actual cheese" that made her uncle violently ill, "but the word alone. It was a conditioned response, like when Pavlov paired a bell with food and subsequently dogs salivated at the sound of a bell."

Young Joan was fascinated with the impact of her uncle's mind on his body. In college, she studied both biology and psychology. When it was time to pick a graduate program, she chose Harvard Medical School. That was the first time she met Benson, who at that time was a young doctor conducting some of the first-ever studies on the power of the mind to influence the body.

After Joan's father died, the two began working together again, eventually creating a mind-body clinic at two Harvard teaching hospitals, "fulfilling the vision of caring for the mental, emotional and spiritual needs of people with stress-related disorders, chronic illness, cancer and HIV/AIDS."

Joan left Harvard as an instructor in medicine in 1988 after her second book, *Minding the Body, Mending the Mind*, became a *New York Times* bestseller. She then began training physicians, psychiatrists, and psychologists in how to integrate spirituality and meaning into health and healing. Now considered a pioneer in the field of integrative medicine, she has written or cowritten seventeen books about health, healing, and spirituality, and she facilitates mind-body programs and retreats all over the world.

"The marriage of science and spirit is my calling card," she said. "The science that continues to intrigue and delight me opened doors that allowed me to share spirituality without losing credibility."

Dear Younger Me,

Life is a grand adventure filled with ups and downs, wins and losses, tears and laughter. If you make kindness, gratitude, and curiosity your primary goals, all the rest will take care of itself. You will attract exactly what you need to live a life of love, joy, and purpose.

CHAPTER SIX

Gail Koziara Boudreaux

HEALTHCARE EXECUTIVE

Gail Koziara Boudreaux. COURTESY OF ELEVANCE HEALTH

FORTUNE MAGAZINE NAMED GAIL KOZIARA BOUDREAUX ONE of its Most Powerful Women in Business; *Forbes* magazine named her one of its Most Powerful Women in the World. She has spent more than three decades as a healthcare industry executive, leading multibillion-dollar companies with her signature combination of strategic problem solving, innovation, and teamwork.

It all began on the basketball court.

As a student-athlete, Gail led the Dartmouth women's basketball team to three consecutive conference championships. She was a four-time All-Ivy League player, and as a senior, she was a third-team All-American. By the time she graduated in 1982, she had been named Ivy League Player of the Year for women's basketball three times—the only woman ever to do so.

To this day, she holds the Dartmouth records for the most points and most rebounds in a single game, a single season, and an entire college career. She remains the school's all-time leading scorer, with 1,933 total points, an average of 21.9 points per game. She's also the school's leading rebounder, with 1,635 rebounds, an average of 18.4 per game.

"By playing sports I learned a great deal that helped me to be successful in business," Gail said in a press release announcing her donation to endow the Dartmouth women's basketball head coach position. "How to be part of a team, how to work hard, how to overcome adversity."[1]

In 1979, Gail got one of her most memorable lessons in teamwork. The sophomore had already established herself as a standout basketball player. But it was a complex season, with upperclassmen often forced to take backup roles because of an unusually talented crop of freshmen and sophomores. Those upperclassmen were sometimes called off the bench for key plays, but they never showed any resentment. They took it all in stride, always keeping the good of the team in mind.

"What I learned from that team is how important it is to get people into the right role, make sure they understand their role as it relates to the team and then support them so they complement their teammates," she said in a 2016 profile on the National Collegiate Athletic Association (NCAA) website.[2]

"It's the same in business," she said. "Even if you have an incredibly talented individual, if they don't buy into the team concept and are not willing to play their role, then you have to swap them out. Everyone isn't a shooter."[3]

Not only was Gail a star basketball player at Dartmouth, she was also a track and field standout, winning four consecutive Ivy League shot put titles and becoming an All-American in the shot put her senior year. She also won the discus throw her junior and senior years, which put her in the top 10 in conference history for total individual titles in women's track and field.

Gail knows firsthand how the qualities of an athlete carry over to the business world. And now that she's in the position of putting together her own teams in the professional arena, she keeps those qualities in mind.

"I've hired a lot of athletes, and what I love about them is that they are willing to take risks, take on challenges, and the good ones understand their role," she said. "The best skill they bring right out of school is the ability to follow, to take guidance, to learn new things and to be part of a bigger project or team."[4]

Gail made the transition from sports to business when she was a senior at Dartmouth, landing a summer internship at Aetna, one of the nation's largest managed health care companies. She entered the company's management training program the following year and rose up the company ranks to become senior vice president.

From there, she took over the helm of Blue Cross and Blue Shield of Illinois, and then, in 2008, she joined UnitedHealthcare as executive vice president. At UnitedHealthcare, she was in charge of sixty thousand employees and $120 billion in revenue, and in 2011, she was promoted to CEO.

In 2017, she became the CEO of Anthem, now called Elevance Health. Gail has led the organization's evolution from a traditional health insurance company to a leader in the industry, which she said reflects her personal commitment to elevating whole health and advancing health beyond healthcare. Elevance Health has more than one hundred thousand employees serving more than 118 million people.

Throughout her career, Gail has been passionate about helping women succeed in the workforce. She not only mentors women in the business world, but she also continues to mentor young basketball players through her alma mater. In 2018, the Women's Sports Foundation recognized her commitment to the success of women in both sports and in the workplace with the Billie Jean King Leadership Award. World tennis champion Billie Jean King presented the award, saying that Gail "has risen to the highest ranks of the global business world because no matter where she is, on the court or in the boardroom, she is a born leader."[5]

Gail's leadership was recognized once again in 2022 with the Theodore Roosevelt Award, the highest honor given by the NCAA. Past winners include four U.S. presidents, astronaut Sally Ride, and former secretary of state Madeleine Albright. The awards committee noted Gail's nationally recognized healthcare leadership during the COVID pandemic.

She said athletics helped her navigate the challenges. "In sports, you learn every game plan is fantastic until someone's defense is better than your offense," she said. "With the pandemic, there's no playbook. It's been a series of challenges like none of us have seen in our lifetimes."[6]

In 2023, Gail achieved another milestone when she was elected chair of the Business Council, a Washington, DC, group comprised of the world's top CEOs. She was the first woman chosen to chair the council in its ninety-year history.

"Gail has been a trailblazer for many years," said Nike CEO John Donahoe, also on the council, "starting with her days as a multi-sport All-American athlete. Throughout her career, she creates real followership wherever she goes. We are fortunate to have her leading the Business Council in the coming years."[7]

Dear Younger Me,

In school, we're taught there is a right answer and a wrong one—and sometimes, there is. But in life, big impact isn't achieved when we perfectly follow directions and look to fit in. Impact is delivered when we bring our whole selves— our beliefs, experiences, talents, and differences—to our work and use them as strengths. Because they are. Be true to yourself and you'll unlock the magic.

CHAPTER SEVEN
Dr. Tara Brach
PSYCHOLOGIST AND MINDFULNESS EXPERT

Dr. Tara Brach. PHOTO BY JONATHAN FOUST, COURTESY OF
DR. TARA BRACH

TARA BRACH, PHD, IS ONE OF THE WORLD'S LEADING EXPERTS on self-compassion. But as a college student, she was her own worst critic.

"My harsh inner judge became really conscious," she said. "I hated myself for overeating and extra weight, condemned myself for falling short academically, as a daughter, and in relationships."[1]

That "pain of feeling unworthy" was one of her primary motivators for seeking out yoga and meditation.[2] At first, her spiritual progress was just another target for self-judgment. But gradually, she realized how all that self-judgment was only amplifying her suffering.

So instead of the path of self-criticism, she chose self-compassion. "I became dedicated to befriending myself," she said, "and this naturally extended to all life. I credit a commitment to mindful self-compassion with being the pivotal place of my emotional healing and spiritual awakening."[3]

Although she was hard on herself in her younger years, Tara has always leaned toward compassion for others. When she was just four years old, her mother was "depressed, anxious and drinking," Tara said. "She tells me that I knew whenever she was upset and regularly tried to comfort her, hugging her, telling her to feel better. In college I became the person to listen to and try to help friends in trouble, and as a young therapist, depression, anxiety, and addiction were at the center of my work."[4]

Now Tara teaches people all over the globe how to be gentle with themselves and others. Her best-selling books have helped people explore their emotional pain, overcome anxiety, and accept their innate worthiness. Her retreats and workshops help people find safe space within themselves. She has trained mindfulness practitioners who have gone on to teach meditation in businesses, government agencies, and prisons. She has also helped launch conflict-resolution programs in schools, supporting educators to create classrooms focused on empathy, where students of all ages participate in activities designed to foster encouragement, mutual respect, and understanding.

No matter the venue, one of Tara's main teachings is to help people become curious about their difficult feelings and welcome them in rather than trying to push them away. She developed a well-known practice called RAIN—an acronym tool for dealing with difficult emotions:

"Recognize what is going on" by making a mental note of what you're thinking, feeling, or experiencing.

"Allow the experience to be there, just as it is," by acknowledging the feeling rather than trying to fix it or avoid it.

"Investigate with interest and care" by tuning in to the feelings as messengers, asking the vulnerable places inside what they need.

"Nurture with self-compassion" by offering messages of kindness and care to the hurt parts of yourself.[5]

Tara's teachings also emphasize the importance of bringing compassion to ourselves and others when we (or they) have lashed out. She often uses the metaphor of someone walking through the woods and seeing a little dog by a tree. When they bend down to pet the dog, it jumps up and bares its fangs, ready to attack. The person immediately goes from feeling friendly toward the dog to feeling angry or afraid, until they see that the dog's paw is caught in a trap. Then they feel sorry for the dog.

When we lash out at someone or when they lash out at us, Tara teaches, it's like having a leg caught in a trap. "People do not cause suffering unless they're suffering in some way," she said. But "being able to see that doesn't mean that I then stand there and let the dog attack me. We still do what we need to do to protect ourselves, but it gives us the quality of heart that lets us respond to the situation in a much more compassionate and intelligent way."[6]

Part of that compassion and intelligence comes from feeling like we're part of a community, Tara said in a 2023 webinar, and from sharing our vulnerabilities. But that sense of connection has dwindled in recent years, creating an "epidemic of loneliness," especially during and after the pandemic. With both children and adults more focused on screens and less focused on community, we've lost our sense of connection to one another, that "soul to soul sense of togetherness" that is so important for our emotional healing and evolution.[7]

"The secret ingredient of a full, happy life is the companionship of kindred spirits," she wrote in an email to her subscribers. "We need each other to learn, grow, awaken, and experience true joy."[8]

Tara's teachings emphasize the importance of holding safe space for one another, free of judgment and criticism, in order to bring back that sense of community, connection, and joy. In order to open up and be authentic, she said, people need to feel like they will be accepted for who they are, rather than judged.

But in order to appreciate others for who they are, we first need to befriend ourselves so we have a framework for what acceptance feels like. And that, she said, takes a lot of slowing down in a world so focused on speeding up. We're a culture focused on *doing*, and Tara wants to shift that to a culture focused on *being*.

One way to create a "non-doing presence," she said, is with a simple twenty-second pause—a "sacred pause"—especially when triggered. While the tendency is to distract ourselves, or to do more, stopping to go inward allows us to "see more, feel more, and respond to our circumstances with more awakeness and open-heartedness . . . that's when we are inhabiting who we really are."[9]

Dear Younger Me,

Trust your basic goodness—the awake and loving aware-ness that is your source. When thoughts of deficiency or personal failure arise, when you feel "something is wrong with me," you don't have to believe your thoughts. Meet the suffering with mindfulness and self-compassion, and you'll reconnect with the truth of your natural being.

CHAPTER EIGHT

Dr. Krystyna Chiger

HOLOCAUST SURVIVOR

Dr. Krystyna Chiger. COURTESY OF DORON KEREN

IT WAS 1941 WHEN THE GERMANS INVADED LVOV, POLAND. They moved into Jewish homes, stole Jewish heirlooms, and forced Jewish families into a crowded, cramped, walled-off ghetto.

Krystyna Chiger was just starting kindergarten.

When the Nazis began storming the ghetto, rounding up Jewish families and taking them to concentration camps, her parents made the heart-wrenching decision to send her to live with a Christian teacher who had offered to shelter the young girl to give her a better chance of surviving the war.

But Krystyna refused. "I remember she was very nice, and she wanted to take me, but I said, 'I'm not going,'" Krystyna recalled. "I told my mother, 'Whatever happens to you will happen to me.' And I meant it. And they could see I was serious. So they listened."[1]

Krystyna's father was among a group of men who began to dig through a concrete floor using forks, spoons, and other small metal tools. Their goal: dig down far enough to reach the underground sewer system so they could escape.

It worked. Right before the final round-up, as the Nazis approached, Krystyna's father and the other men made it underground.

But they were shocked to see a Polish sewer worker standing there. His name was Leopold Socha, and he was equally shocked to see the men. He was, however, impressed that they had managed to dig a hole through the concrete basement floor.

So they brokered a deal. Krystyna's father and the others would pay Socha for helping them survive in the sewer.

Krystyna, her mother, and her brother were still above ground in the basement when Socha climbed up a makeshift ladder and surprised them.

"This is it," said Krystyna's mother, Pepa. "We're done for!"[2]

But then Socha broke out into a big smile and told them he was going to help save their lives.

Krystyna, her family, and a group of other Jewish refugees crawled down into the sewer just in time. Underground, they braved flash flooding, fires, and the constant, nearly unbearable stench of sewage. They watched helplessly as some members of their group disappeared in the strong currents and died from disease. They were forced to sleep on stones covered in worms. To avoid detection from the Nazis above, who were still searching for them, they could never speak above a whisper.

They managed to hide for fourteen harrowing months with the help of Socha, who risked his life to keep them fed and protected. The Nazis made it clear that they would kill anyone found to be sheltering or helping Jewish people.

"He was our angel," Krystyna recalled, "and our light. Always look for a light in the tunnel. He was ours. People like this exist among us, beautiful human beings who are willing to sacrifice everything to keep others safe."

Socha kept them apprised of troop movements above, moved them to more secure locations within the sewer system when the Nazis began to suspect where they were hiding, and brought them bread, which was often stolen by the giant rats that also lived in the sewer system.

When it rained, the water level in the sewer would climb so high that Krystyna's parents had to hoist her and her younger brother up, holding them higher than the water line to keep them from drowning.

From her hiding place underground, Krystyna could hear cars, music, and other sounds above. She could hear children's happy voices. She could hear them laughing and singing and playing. She remembers thinking how happy she would have been to be able to play freely like those children she was hearing above. But instead, she spent her next birthday in silence, bitterly cold in the underground maze, suffering from sickness.

Krystyna recalled one particular conversation between a young girl and her mother just above a storm drain. They were buying flowers from a street vendor. "I love flowers," Krystyna recalled, "and my mother knew it. She promised me that someday we would be free, and we would buy flowers."

And then, more than a year after they first crawled down into the sewer system, Krystyna and her family were free. The sewer worker who had helped keep them alive came down to tell them the war was over.

"I couldn't believe it," she said. "I just couldn't believe we were free."

Her little brother Pavel was terrified when he emerged from the sewer, because he wasn't used to daylight.

"He wanted to go back down to the only world he knew," Krystyna said. "I remember him pulling on my mother's coat because he was so shocked from all the light and wanted to go back to the darkness he was used to."

Of the 150,000 Jews who lived in Lvov, only three families survived the war, including Krystyna's.

She recounted her experience in a memoir, *The Girl in the Green Sweater*. To keep warm in the sewer, she wore a green sweater knit by her grandmother, which she kept on the entire time she was in hiding. It is now on display at the United States Holocaust Memorial Museum. The family's ordeal was also the subject of a Polish film *In Darkness*, nominated for Best Foreign Language Film at the 84th Academy Awards.

When the Chigers emerged from the sewer and out into the world, Krystyna received a yellow gooseberry fruit from a street vendor.

"I remember holding it," she said, "and I just felt it was such a symbol of life."[3]

Dear Younger Me,

Never lose hope.

CHAPTER NINE

María Soledad Cisternas Reyes

LAWYER AND
DISABILITY RIGHTS ADVOCATE

María Soledad Cisternas Reyes. COURTESY OF MARÍA SOLEDAD
CISTERNAS REYES

WHEN MARÍA SOLEDAD CISTERNAS REYES WAS FOURTEEN years old, she was diagnosed with a rare eye disease called retinitis, which causes inflammation of the tissue in the back of the eye. It's a degenerative disease, and María's vision grew progressively worse.

She was determined to attend college, though, where she studied law, hiding her worsening vision from her classmates and teachers. Eventually, she couldn't hide it anymore, and she became blind.

And although she had a difficult time accepting her blindness, it was the catalyst that brought her life's work into focus: a career dedicated to championing the rights of people with disabilities all over the world.

In 2017, the UN secretary general appointed María to the position of special envoy on disability and accessibility, putting her in charge of ensuring that people with disabilities have equal access to society. Before that, she was the chair of the UN Committee on the Rights of Persons with Disabilities.

Trained as a human rights lawyer, María began her disability rights advocacy in 1998, when she sued a Chilean airline for making her fly with either a nondisabled co-traveler or a guide dog, at her own expense. The courts ruled against her.

But that loss turned out to be a win. María petitioned the Inter-American Commission on Human Rights, which forced the two sides to the negotiating table.

"I sat across the table from numerous civil aviation representatives and regulators, where I had the opportunity to explain the discriminatory nature of their conduct and the need for legal protections against it," María wrote in an article for the Harvard Law School journal the *Practice*.[1]

Five years later, the commission approved a settlement agreement, which included María's appointment to the Air

Traffic Control Commission in Chile. That settlement, she wrote, "vindicated my earlier losses and resulted in positive changes to Chile's air traffic regulations that expanded access for passengers with disabilities."[2]

And the wins kept coming. María created a new program at a Chilean law school where she organized seminars and activities to raise awareness about disability rights. She also organized trainings for judges on the importance of, and methods for, incorporating disability rights into legal decisions.

She also partnered with law school clinics to bring more disability rights cases before the courts, including one case that challenged the lack of accessibility in public transportation, and another case that challenged the lack of sign language interpreters in news broadcasts.

In both cases, the courts ruled against her. But yet again, María turned those losses into wins, highlighting the legal lack of protections for people with disabilities.

Because of María's persistence and advocacy efforts, transportation officials commissioned studies to find gaps in accessibility in the bus system. They incorporated new standards based on those studies.

And the television case raised awareness about the barriers people with disabilities face in accessing television broadcasts. There were public protests and roundtable discussions with TV station executives, which resulted in an agreement to include sign language interpretation in news broadcasts. That agreement later became law.

"My experience with these cases has shown that losses in court can nevertheless lead to positive changes," María wrote. "Indeed, unfavorable court decisions can mobilize civil society organizations to raise public awareness, and these awareness-raising campaigns may later bring about the same aims that the litigant sought to achieve through the courts."[3]

During the presidential election of 2005 in Chile, María brought another unsuccessful case against a district that had prevented a blind person from voting with the help of an assistant. The case prompted her to start an advocacy campaign that included TV ads featuring people with disabilities along with workshops and trainings for municipal officials and election workers.

María's campaign was so successful that it led to sweeping election reforms with better accessibility requirements. From then on, people with disabilities were legally granted the right to voting assistance.

For María, being an effective human-rights lawyer means also fighting and advocating outside the courtroom.

"I believe that a disability cause lawyer's duties are not confined to securing a positive judicial decision," she wrote. "Rather, they encompass a broader responsibility to guarantee rights in ways that generate changes for the widest number of persons with disabilities possible. . . . Over time, disability cause lawyers who possess a special kind of conviction and persistence have the power to change their countries' legal systems."[4]

Because of that conviction and persistence, María was honored by the American Bar Association (ABA) in 2022 with its International Human Rights Award, calling her "a true pioneer in the field of international human rights law and a champion of the most vulnerable populations across the world."[5]

ABA president Deborah Enix-Ross said that María "deserves all the accolades for her career-long, transformative advocacy for the rights of persons with disabilities—precisely the kind of dedication and effectiveness the ABA International Human Rights Award was established to recognize."[6]

Dear Younger Me,

I'm so pleased watching that you, being so young, have had justice as the inspiring principle of your life, and that you already have started a path inspired by those who need justice in their life. Keep embracing those values that will lead you to the contribution of a big legacy to leave behind. I'm also very proud to see that you have become a strong defender of human rights, able to distinguish good from bad. In this way, you will walk confidently through life, knowing that you have not harmed anyone, because you have been consistent with your ideals. Your studies, independence, convictions, humility, and honesty are the keys to go through life with spiritual satisfaction. You can't go wrong if you care and love your family. Always value being a woman with all that this word implies, because we must face multiple challenges. Try very hard to balance your efforts and your spare time, so that the first ones don't exceed the last ones. Overextending yourself, even with convictions, can affect your body and mind. Love yourself a lot!

CHAPTER TEN

Dr. Dianne Chong

AEROSPACE ENGINEER

Dr. Dianne Chong. COURTESY OF DR. DIANNE CHONG

Dianne Chong, PhD, has headed up technological advances at the world's biggest aerospace company. Now retired but still active in the engineering community, she was vice president of research and technology at Boeing, which designs and produces airplanes, military defense systems, satellites, rockets, and telecommunications equipment.

Boeing is also America's biggest manufacturing exporter, and Dianne's work on special projects has impacted government allies in more than 150 countries. Before she was named Boeing's vice president of research and technology, Dianne was vice president of materials, manufacturing, structures, and support at the company.

But even though Dianne has held top management positions, her leadership philosophy is opposite from what one might expect.

"Instead of having an organization chart that is the standard pyramid where the leader is at the top and all the people are at the bottom," she said, "you turn it upside down and the people are all at the top and the leader (myself) is at the bottom. When you have that kind of perspective on the organization, it can help a leader understand the people's needs."[1]

As a leader, Dianne was known for understanding people's needs. She set up an online forum where employees could discuss their concerns. She set up engagement teams to represent the "hearts and minds of the people."[2]

Their mission was to let Dianne know how she could be a better leader, how she could accommodate their needs, and how she could build their trust. She responded to their comments with the compassionate overall message that "I can't promise I'll do everything you want me to do, but I will listen carefully to your concerns."[3]

Dianne emphasizes the importance of listening to, and respecting, everyone. From different perspectives come different ideas, she said. And that leads to innovation.

"Ideas come from everywhere, all around the world," Dianne said. "It's not just the researchers in our company or the researchers outside the company, it can come from anywhere. . . . Experienced people who are practitioners at engineering, people who are on the shop floor can introduce great ideas to us."[4]

At Boeing, Dianne said, it was also important to her to let people know they were valued. When people feel their intrinsic worth, they're more likely to take risks and come up with out-of-the-box solutions.

"People want to innovate, whether it's something to do with the technology that we're working at, an approach to problem-solving, or even organizational structure," she said. "People have approached me with great suggestions about innovation relative to technology, organizational structure, employee health, safety and emotional resilience. Many of these ideas were implemented into programs that benefited our employees."[5]

Dianne is active in promoting inclusion and equal opportunity for minorities in science and engineering. In 2007, she was elected the first-ever female president of the professional scientific organization ASM International. She serves on the steering committee of Engineer Girl, a program of the National Academy of Engineering.

She loves talking to young women about the field of engineering. And while she encourages students to seek out mentors, she said it goes both ways—she also encourages leaders from all disciplines to talk to students.

"I think the best thing that female leaders can do is go out and talk to young women who haven't made up their mind about what they want to do," she said. "It's important to transmit that sense of passion and inspire others."[6]

Dianne's primary source of inspiration was her mother, a Chinese immigrant who was widowed at an early age, leaving her to support five children on her own. Dianne, the oldest, was thirteen when her father died.

"My mother demonstrated strength," Dianne said, "and having a strong value system . . . no matter how poor we were, she would always help the neighbors as well. She was always kind-hearted and did whatever she could."[7]

Dianne said she also learned "RAA" from her mother: "Responsibility, authority and accountability. This helped me in developing some of the leadership skills I used later."[8]

In high school, Dianne planned to be a physician. When she got to college, she decided to double major in biology and psychology. "I think this is where the understanding people and how to develop mutual respect was reinforced," she said.[9] While she was getting her PhD in physiological psychology, her youngest brother, a mechanical engineer, told her he thought she should consider engineering because she enjoyed solving problems in a certain way and seeing the immediate results. She started taking engineering courses, she loved them, and she ended up getting her PhD in engineering.

When asked for her opinion on the most important trait in a leader, Dianne said, "Integrity. I think leaders have to be open and honest and always make solid decisions, but they have to have integrity while making these decisions and leading their workforce."[10]

Dear Younger Me,

I know that you had a lot of responsibility thrust upon you at an early age, since your father passed away when you were only thirteen. As a first-born, first-generation Chinese American, you were expected to help your widowed mother and younger brothers and sisters. This may lead to what is actually important—you or the outcomes. If you focus on the former, you may become too single-minded in your work. By focusing on the latter, you can open your mind to more creative and diverse solutions.

CHAPTER ELEVEN

Dr. Johnnetta Betsch Cole

ANTHROPOLOGIST, COLLEGE PRESIDENT, AND MUSEUM DIRECTOR

Dr. Johnnetta Betsch Cole. PHOTO BY BOSTON PHOTOGRAPHY, LLC, AMELIA ISLAND, FLORIDA

As a child living in the segregated South, Johnnetta Cole was constantly reminded where she wasn't allowed to go. "One of my biggest challenges," she said, "was the ubiquitous signs that said, 'This water or bathroom or school library or swimming pool or part of the bus were not for me.'"[1]

When she was five years old, she crossed over into a whites-only neighborhood, where a boy attacked her with racial slurs.

But rather than perpetuating the pain of exclusion, Johnnetta has dedicated her life to raising awareness about the impact of discrimination and making the world a more inclusive place.

One of her earliest role models was her great-grandfather, Abraham Lincoln Lewis. He had only an elementary school education, but he cofounded the Afro-American Life Insurance Company in 1901 and went on to become the first Black millionaire in the state of Florida. In 1935, he cofounded American Beach in Nassau County as a vacation destination for Black Americans who weren't allowed to go to other beaches because of segregation. He strongly encouraged Johnnetta to get an education and pursue public service.

When she was only fifteen years old, Johnnetta enrolled at Fisk University in Tennessee. She went on to earn her master's degree and PhD in anthropology from Northwestern University in Illinois.

In 1962, Johnnetta went from student to teacher, becoming a professor at Washington State University, where she started the country's first African American Studies program. She then moved on to the University of Massachusetts at Amherst, where she created that college's first African American Studies department.

Another milestone came in 1987, when Johnnetta became the first Black female president of Spelman College, a liberal arts school founded to educate women of African descent. She led Spelman to a #1 *U.S. News and World Report* ranking for liberal arts colleges in the South. It was the first time a historically Black college received a #1 ranking. But Johnnetta wasn't done breaking barriers. During her tenure at Spelman, she earned a spot on the board of directors of Coca-Cola, the first woman ever to do so.

After a decade leading Spelman, Johnnetta became a Presidential Distinguished Professor of Anthropology, Women's Studies and African American Studies at Emory University. From there, she accepted her second college presidency, this time at Bennett College in North Carolina. This made her the only person ever to serve as president of the country's two historically Black women's colleges.

As a pioneer in academia, inclusion, and public service, Johnnetta emphasized the importance of those qualities in a video message to young people. The organization Scholarship America awarded her a Lifetime Achievement Honor in 2021, releasing a video that featured her telling students that education "is how you will not only learn about your own history and culture, you will learn about the history and culture of people who are different from you."[2]

The video, called *Dear Young Students: An Open Letter from Dr. Johnnetta Cole*, also highlighted the importance of service. "I was taught that doing for others is the rent you've got to pay for your room on earth," she said. "Whether I'm engaging in a simple act of kindness, or an ongoing service activity, what I am doing for others, it comes back to me tenfold, in the form of a mighty good feeling."[3]

Johnnetta also spoke about the importance of courage, telling students that "it takes courage to speak up when you witness someone being attacked because of their race, gender, sexual orientation, religion, disability or any other identity. . . . It takes courage to be your authentic self, rather than doing what others are doing, when if you do, it is a violation of who you are. . . . May you always be of service to others, and may you always have the courage to do what you know is the right thing to do."[4]

After retiring from academia, Johnnetta became the director of the Smithsonian Institution's National Museum of African Art, where she established the first-ever chief diversity officer position at a Smithsonian museum. She began working in earnest for greater inclusion in the nation's museums.

In 2015, Johnnetta gave the keynote speech at a meeting of the American Alliance of Museums, where she talked about the importance of increasing diversity in museum staff, visitors, exhibits, and leadership.

"Like all African Americans who grew up in the pre–civil rights days of legal segregation in the South," she said, "I went to colored schools, used the colored public library, and only drank from the colored water fountains, forced always to sit in the back of the bus."[5]

Black people weren't allowed to visit museums, she said, but her mother filled the family's home with African American art and books. "Today, with legalized segregation a thing of the past," she said, "I can go to any museum whose entrance fee, if there is one, I can afford. And yet too often, I will not find much in those museums which reflects the history—the *her*story—the culture, and the art of who I am."[6]

She called on America's museums to create more diversity in not only exhibits, but also in management. "I can't stress enough," she said, "the importance of an inclusive culture that says, in countless ways, all colleagues from all backgrounds are welcome at this museum table."[7]

In 2018, Johnnetta became president of the National Council of Negro Women. In 2021, President Joe Biden awarded her the National Humanities Medal for her leadership in the area of racial inclusion.

Johnnetta's trailblazing work was honored the following year with an ATHENA International Global Award, which recognizes "the torchbearers and trailblazers who have personified professional excellence in amplifying the importance of giving women a voice of empowerment."[8] Past recipients include the late US Supreme Court justice Ruth Bader Ginsburg, former secretary of state Condoleezza Rice, and tennis great Billie Jean King.

In presenting the award, Traci Corey, president and CEO of ATHENA International, said that Johnnetta's "trailblazing work and exemplary accomplishments embody everything ATHENA International has represented in advancing and empowering women leaders throughout the world."[9]

Dear Younger Me,

You will often have to be twice as good to get half as far as people who are not African American girls. But as long as you keep the faith, believe in yourself, do your best in school, and always help others who need you, you are going to have a very special life. So go on and soar to the height of your possibilities!

CHAPTER TWELVE
Ertharin Cousin
LAWYER AND ANTI-HUNGER ADVOCATE

Ertharin Cousin. OFFICIAL GOVERNMENT PHOTO

Ertharin Cousin has never forgotten the scream she heard when she walked into a refugee camp in Kenya. It was "a scream that could only be a mother's cry of loss," she said, "a scream that could only be a mother's pain." This mother had walked more than six hundred miles with her children, from Somalia to Kenya, in search of food. "By the time she reached the refugee camp," Ertharin said, "her youngest child was dying, and all she could do was scream."[1]

Ertharin has dedicated her life and career to helping people like that mother, who was forced to watch helplessly as her six-month-old baby died from malnourishment and dehydration.

"It is possible to stop these mothers from walking," she said. "We can break the cycle of hunger. . . . Close your eyes for a minute. Visualize a world where every mother everywhere has everything she needs to feed her children. You can see it, can't you?"[2]

Ertharin is committed to turning that visualization into reality. Known as "the woman who feeds the world," she has headed up global hunger-relief efforts since 1997, when President Bill Clinton appointed her to the Board of Agriculture and International Development, which advises the government on food insecurity.

From there, she joined the board of America's Second Harvest/Feeding America, the country's largest hunger-relief organization. She climbed the ranks to become its executive vice president and chief operating officer, supporting the operations of two hundred food banks across the country that serve more than 50 million meals every year. During her tenure there, Hurricane Katrina struck the Gulf Coast, leaving thousands of people without food. Because of Ertharin's leadership, 62 million pounds of food reached the hurricane victims.

In 2009, President Barack Obama appointed her the United States ambassador to the United Nations Agencies for Food and Agriculture in Rome, Italy, where she helped various countries set up hunger-relief programs. When a catastrophic earthquake struck Haiti in 2010, Ertharin was instrumental in getting emergency relief food to people in need.

Forbes magazine named her one of its Most Powerful Women, *Time* magazine named her one of its 100 Most Influential People, and *Foreign Policy* magazine listed her as one of its 500 Most Powerful People on the Planet.

But to Ertharin, helping to feed hungry people means more than accolades or titles.

"The biggest trap you can fall into as you experience opportunities that allow you to serve in a higher position," she said, "is to begin to define yourself by that title, by that position. And so having the ability to continue to be me and then to help people in a way that's beyond my title, but it's Ertharin who's helping you. . . . That makes me feel good."[3]

Ertharin grew up in a low-income neighborhood in Chicago. She learned at an early age the importance of helping the people who needed it most. After school, she would help out at her grandmother's restaurant. When people came in who couldn't afford meals, her grandmother would give them food free of charge.

Ertharin's mother was a social worker and her father was an activist in their community, so she was raised in an environment of service. She was also raised to believe in herself and her ability to create change.

"I was born into a family with a mother and father who believed that their daughters should grow up with no ceilings on their dreams," she said, "who encouraged us to want more, to outrun the boys, to not be afraid to jump higher. What you have doesn't limit what you do."[4]

In 2012, Ertharin brought her fight to end hunger onto an even bigger global stage when the U.S. State Department announced that she would be the executive director of the United Nations World Food Programme, the world's largest humanitarian organization fighting food insecurity. Her leadership there was instrumental in getting a $2 billion increase in funding for vouchers and other government programs to help support access to nutritious food for the world's most vulnerable people.

Still, she believes that both the public and private sectors should be doing more to help hungry families help themselves. Her advocacy efforts extend to areas like boosting crop storage capabilities, technological tools, and refrigeration and transportation systems for small farmers, who are often forced to throw away food because they can't afford to get it to the people who need it most.

Ertharin also advocates for policies and laws to make sure corporations pay their workers fair wages, so those workers can afford to feed their families. These policies, she said, build resilience, helping people help themselves.

But world hunger policies are geared more toward emergencies, she said, than building self-sufficiency: "We're not moved by the idea of providing resilience; we're moved by the pictures of starving babies and women walking, and so we feed the same people every year."[5]

During her tenure at the United Nations World Food Programme, Ertharin said, "we didn't take pictures of babies with flies on their eyes and bloated bellies. We took pictures of fat, healthy babies because I wanted people to see that in the worst places in the world, babies can thrive when we provide them with the assistance that is necessary."[6]

Dear Younger Me,

Your hard work and preparation will indeed pay off over time. Relax! Don't miss the joy of today.

Love,
Older, Happier, and Wiser Me

CHAPTER THIRTEEN

Melinda Emerson

ENTREPRENEUR

Melinda Emerson. PHOTO BY JASEN HUDSON, COURTESY OF
MELINDA EMERSON

MELINDA EMERSON WAKES UP EVERY MORNING WITH THE help of a clock. It's not an alarm clock, though.

"I have a purpose clock," she said. "My mission is to end small business failure."[1]

Back in 2007, Melinda was the owner of a struggling marketing business. Her marriage was ending, and she was on bed rest with a high-risk pregnancy. She was miserable. But she had a passion for helping people and a vision that she would one day teach people all over the country how to succeed in business. She used her time on bed rest to start writing a book called *Become Your Own Boss in 12 Months*.

But the following year, when the book was scheduled for publication, the world experienced the Global Financial Crisis—the worst economic crisis since the Great Depression. The stock market and housing market crashed, and Melinda's publisher postponed the launch of her book by a year and a half. She was devastated. But she took the advice of a friend, who suggested she hire a publicist to begin promoting the book, even though it wouldn't be coming out until 2010.

That publicist suggested that Melinda begin building an author platform on Twitter. But when she went to sign up for a Twitter account, she discovered that her name, Melinda Emerson, was already taken.

"After I got over the initial shock," she said, "my publicist suggested that we come up with a nickname that would tell people who I am and what I am about. We came up with *SmallBizLady*, which we now know was the best branding move ever."[2]

Part of Melinda's brand was her mission: to end small business failure. She used that brand and that mission to build a social media empire that now reaches 3 million small business owners every week. As the CEO of Quintessence Group,

Melinda not only helps small businesses grow, she also advises *Fortune* 500 companies on how to market to small business owners. Her clients include corporations like Visa, FedEx, Google, Sam's Club, and IKEA.

She has a blog with thousands of articles, a weekly podcast that broadcasts business advice live across various social media channels, and #SmallBizChat, the longest-running live chat on Twitter for small business owners, which prompted *Forbes* magazine in 2010 to name her the #1 woman for entrepreneurs to follow on Twitter.

That same year, *Black Enterprise* magazine called her newly released book "the best start-up book they ever read. I cried when I read the review," she said. "It was such validation."[3]

She also has an online school for women and minorities trying to find a way out of the corporate world and into entrepreneurship. Teaching is one of her passions. She's an adjunct professor at Drexel University, her alma mater, and she also mentors female business leaders just starting on their path to entrepreneurship. She wants her journey to inspire the next generation of small business owners.

"I want to help young entrepreneurs benefit from my hard-learned lessons in business," Melinda said. "I love sharing my secrets to success."[4]

One of those secrets to success is an acronym: HELP. She advises her clients to use it as a mantra in their social media strategy.

"H stands for provide Helpful content, E stands for Engage with people personally, L stands for Listen carefully—each social media site is different, don't assume you know the culture of each social media site—P stands for Promote yourself with care. Be sure to spend the time building relationships online; no one wants to be sold to."[5]

Another success secret Melinda likes to pass on is the value of teamwork. "Any business is only as strong as its team's processes," she said. "In a strong company, anyone can be empowered to be a leader, even an intern."[6]

Empowering people to lead, Melinda has learned, requires the intentional creation of an environment that is "nurturing and fun, with a clear sense of purpose and a commitment to excellence. You need to be kind and thoughtful as a leader, and that will set an example for everyone else."[7]

Melinda also hopes to lead by example in the area of boundaries. She takes care not to blur the line between her personal and professional life, and she earmarks specific hours for work. She doesn't answer client calls or emails during her dedicated home time, she schedules social media content in advance, and she doesn't allow anyone in her family to use their phone at the dinner table.

This work/life balance is especially important for women, she said, since a lot of women-owned businesses were hurt by the pandemic and their owners have been struggling with how to incorporate more digital resources while maintaining joy in their life.

"Women need to support other women in business," Melinda said. "Women business owners need to hire women, mentor younger women and do business with other women and remember that every relationship is, 'Give to Get.'"[8]

Dear Younger Me,

You are already enough. Everything you need is already in you. Don't let anyone else's opinion become more important than yours.

CHAPTER FOURTEEN
Mackenzie Feldman
ENVIRONMENTAL ACTIVIST

Mackenzie Feldman. PHOTO BY WILL BRINKERHOFF, COURTESY OF
MACKENZIE FELDMAN

When Mackenzie Feldman showed up one morning in the spring of 2017 for her University of California, Berkeley beach volleyball practice, the coach warned the team members not to chase after any balls if they rolled off the court. Why? Groundskeepers had just sprayed an herbicide a few minutes before.

Mackenzie was concerned. In class, she had learned about toxic herbicides like glyphosate, a known carcinogen also linked to a host of diseases and disorders, including Alzheimer's, Parkinson's, depression, endocrine disruption, ADHD, and liver disease. When Mackenzie and one of her teammates contacted the athletic grounds manager to find out what had been sprayed on the court, he told them it was indeed a product containing 41 percent glyphosate.

"Finding out that the herbicide was sprayed around the court was such an important moment in my life," she said. "Maybe it seems weird to think of it this way, but I am so grateful for that moment, because it felt like a clear, guiding message from something or someone greater than myself that this is the work I am being called on to do. If you're lucky, you get a few moments in your life that feel almost like you are remembering decisions instead of making them. This moment was one of those."[1]

From that moment on, Mackenzie made it her mission to get the chemical banned from the beach volleyball court. The grounds manager told her he didn't have the staff needed to pick the weeds by hand, so she recruited all the women on her team to do it. They had regular weeding days before practice. But she didn't stop there.

Once she got synthetic herbicides banned from the beach volleyball court, she moved on to the rest of the campus. She worked with the student government to form an herbicide-free team, and by the time she graduated in 2018, she had expanded the campaign to include all the University of California (UC) campuses. It wasn't easy. She encountered hesitant administrators, budget battles, and other roadblocks. But she kept at it, educating people on the dangers of pesticides and the importance of maintaining healthy, organic soil and plants. Because of her efforts, all ten schools in the UC system banned glyphosate.

"I had been wanting to be a part of big change for a long time," she said, "and this felt like the opportunity where I could finally start to be a part of that."

She found a high-profile ally in a man named Lee Johnson. He was a former groundskeeper who developed cancer after years of working with glyphosate-based herbicides. The year after she graduated from college, Mackenzie sat in on his trial. He was suing the chemical giant Monsanto for failing to warn of the cancer-causing danger of Roundup, a weed killer that contains glyphosate.

"Sitting in his trial, I was enraged as I listened to the Monsanto lawyer talk about how Lee didn't get cancer from Roundup, as Lee sat there with lesions all over his body, dying from cancer," Mackenzie said. "But sometimes there are these rare moments of light that come through the cracks of darkness."

She followed her intuition, wrote Lee a letter saying how inspired she was by his courage to stand up to Monsanto, and told him about her campaign to ban herbicides. She left her email address and passed the letter to his lawyer. A few weeks later, after Lee won his historic case, he emailed Mackenzie and asked how he could be part of her campaign.

"I am grateful that the rage I have toward Monsanto/Bayer inspired me to write Lee that letter," she said. Mackenzie invited Lee and his family to her home state of Hawaii as part of an effort to teach groundskeepers, educators, and policy-makers about the dangers of pesticides. As a result, the Hawaii Department of Education banned herbicides from every public school in the state.

Meanwhile, Mackenzie was expanding her campaign to other schools and universities around the country, including Princeton, Brandeis, Emory, and many others, with her newly formed nonprofit Herbicide-Free Campus. She began helping college students organize their own teams to change policies on herbicide and pesticide use.

Mackenzie and her nonprofit—now called Re:wild Your Campus—continue to educate and empower students and groundskeepers nationwide to eliminate toxic chemicals from school grounds and convert to organic. She also guides schools on how to include native plants that can absorb the carbon that contributes to climate change.

Dear Younger Me,

Pay attention to what makes you different. These gifts will guide you on a career path you will never imagine, so trust your gut and don't stress about what you are going to do with your life. And remember, no matter how passionate you are about your work, your self-worth is not tied to your accomplishments. And finally, it's just as important to enjoy the land as it is to work hard to save it. So take a deep breath, get outside, learn about your ancestors, talk to farm-ers, try not to be overwhelmed by the state of the world, find delight in every day, and know that you will not see the end result of your work, and that's okay.

CHAPTER FIFTEEN

Dr. Christine Figgener

MARINE CONSERVATION BIOLOGIST

Dr. Christine Figgener. PHOTO BY ANDREY MACCARTHY, COUR-
TESY OF DR. CHRISTINE FIGGENER

IN 2015, DR. CHRISTINE FIGGENER, INTERNATIONALLY known as "the sea turtle biologist," was leading a research team in the water off Costa Rica. She was studying the endangered olive ridley sea turtle and collecting genetic data for her PhD.

When Christine spotted a male sea turtle swimming near the surface and brought him on board the boat, she had no idea that he was about to become, as she put it, "the poster turtle" for the extreme harm that single-use plastics can inflict on marine life, or that together, they were about to galvanize the global movement to ban plastic straws.[1]

Christine and her colleagues immediately noticed that the turtle had something stuck in his nose. They thought it might be a barnacle. He was in severe distress—hissing, crying, and having trouble breathing. When one of Christine's colleagues began pulling the object out of the turtle's nose, it kept coming. It was longer than they thought. It appeared to be jammed so tightly, they thought it might be attached to the turtle's brain. Blood was dripping from the sea turtle's nose. This was no barnacle. They thought maybe it was a worm.

But then they noticed the object had faded stripes.

"Don't tell me it's a straw," Christine said.[2] She had spent her career trying to warn the world about the dangers of single-use plastics and how harmful they could be to sea turtles and other animals.

When they finally managed to remove the object, the team made a startling discovery: It was indeed a plastic straw that had become lodged inside the turtle's nasal cavity. Christine surmised that the turtle had swallowed the straw, thinking it was food. When he tried to regurgitate it, she thought, the straw likely became stuck. Based on the degradation of the straw, it had probably been stuck there, hampering the turtle's breathing, for several weeks. When the team was certain the sea turtle's breathing had returned to normal, they set him free. Christine said everyone on the boat was silent as they watched him swim away.

And then Christine got to work warning the world about the dangers of plastic straws.

She had recorded the whole rescue operation, and she uploaded the video to YouTube. It went viral and has since been viewed more than 180 million times. Christine began doing interviews with global media outlets on the impacts of single-use plastics on marine life. Her efforts prompted cities, states, companies, and businesses to enact "offer first" straw policies, replace them with safer alternatives, or ban them outright.

Although straws represent only a fraction of the problem, Christine said, they are a gateway to increasing awareness about the dangers of plastics polluting the world's oceans, and they're a way to ease people in to breaking their single-use plastics habit. Her efforts earned her the position of science and education director for the Footprint Foundation, a global nonprofit working to educate people about the health and environmental dangers of single-use plastics. In announcing Christine's role with the organization, Footprint CEO Troy Swope hailed her as casting "a floodlight on the damaging effects of plastic pollution" and said she brings "both extensive scientific knowledge of the plastic waste crisis impact on marine life and a deep desire to change the world."[3]

In 2018, three years after her video went viral, Christine was named a Next Generation Leader by *Time* magazine. She continues to work with the next generation to raise awareness about the dangers of plastics in the ocean and the importance of protecting sea turtles. She mentors students and young scientists around the world. She visits classrooms in person and virtually. She works with budding environmentalists to eliminate single-use plastics like straws and utensils from school cafeterias.

One middle school student in California, Chloe Mei Espinosa, was so moved after watching the video that she launched her own campaign to ban straws, convincing her thirty-two-campus school district to stop using plastic straws. "Christine's efforts inspire me to never give up protecting our ocean," Chloe Mei said.[4]

For Christine, working with students is rewarding in itself, but doubly so because children pass the information on to their parents. "If we really want to change something," Christine said, "we need to talk to the next generation."[5]

She's also talking to the next generation about what it's like to be a woman in the traditionally male-dominated STEM field, mentoring young women with an interest in science and encouraging them to pursue related careers.

The year after she recorded the video of the sea turtle and the straw, Christine filmed another viral video—this one showing a sea turtle tangled in fishing gear—which helped raise awareness about the dangers of discarded nets.

"I love my turtles so much," she said. "I want to help prepare a habitat for them where they can live safely for the future."[6]

Dear Younger Me,

You have a powerful voice. Always remember that. Use it to speak on behalf of those who have no voice.

CHAPTER SIXTEEN

Beth Ford

BUSINESS EXECUTIVE

Beth Ford. PHOTO COURTESY OF LAND O'LAKES, INC.

When Beth Ford was twelve years old, she spent her summer detasseling corn for $2 an hour. It was her first job, and she got up early every morning to take a bus to the Iowa cornfields. She grew up in a working-class family. Her father was a truck driver, her mother was a nurse, and both of them instilled in their eight children a strong work ethic.

"You had to work for what you got," she told the *New York Times*. "If you wanted to go to college, you have to figure out a way to pay your way."[1]

In fact, Beth worked her way through college as a convenience store cashier, a house painter, and a janitor. "I cleaned toilets," she said. "When you're in that, you don't think, 'Oh this is great.' But now I reflect back on that and say: 'What a blessing. How wonderful is that?'"[2]

Beth carried that work ethic with her through Iowa State University and Columbia Business School, landing jobs at seven different companies spanning six industries. In 2011, she was working in New York with no intention of going back to the Midwest. But she was intrigued by the cooperative model at Land O'Lakes, a member-owned agricultural cooperative founded in 1921 by a group of dairy farmers in Minnesota and one of America's leading food companies.

She learned more about the cooperative model in her interview and was sold on the notion of farmers coming together to feed the world's growing population. "What an opportunity to make a real impact," she thought, and she took the job as chief supply chain and operations officer at Land O'Lakes.[3]

She was eventually promoted to chief operations officer and continued to rise up the ranks to chief executive officer in 2018, becoming not only the company's first female CEO but also the first openly gay female CEO of a *Fortune* 500 company.

It was a milestone hailed by the LGBTQ+ community, especially since Beth was hired as an out lesbian. "This is not a story of someone getting into the higher echelons of leadership and then coming out," said Deena Fidas, director of workplace equality at the Human Rights Campaign, in an interview with CNN Business. "This is someone walking into this role with her full self."[4]

And although Beth emphasized that the Land O'Lakes board chose the person they thought could best lead the company, regardless of sexual orientation, she also said she embraces being a role model for gay women in business. "I made a decision long ago to live an authentic life and if my being named CEO helps others do the same, that's a wonderful moment," she said.[5]

Part of being authentic, Beth said, is having the courage to show up in the world and be seen, without feeling the need to hide the truth of who you are.

"Visibility is what is critical," she said. "I think it's about showing up, doing your best work, being your best self, and being visible. That encourages authenticity, no matter whether you're gay or not."[6]

But visibility, she said, doesn't mean needing to be in the spotlight. In fact, one of the hallmarks of a successful leader is the willingness to put together a team of people whose input and ideas are accepted and valued.

"I believe the biggest secret to my success is that I hire very smart people and I work with very smart people, and I don't need to be the star of that conversation," she said. "If somebody else has a better answer, that's terrific. I'm all about that. I think the team is critical to put you in a position to succeed."[7]

And success, Beth said, can come only if you're willing to risk failure. Because with failure comes the opportunity to grow.

"I fear sometimes that some young women I've spoken to are concerned to step out because they're afraid of failure. That is part of life," she said. "Resilience allows you to learn the lesson and say, 'I'm not going to wear that as an anchor around my neck, I'm going to move forward.'"[8]

Beth has been named a Best Leader by *Fast Company* magazine, and *Fortune* magazine listed her as one of its World's 50 Greatest Leaders and Most Powerful Women. In an interview with *Fortune*, she shared her definition of what it means to be powerful.

"A powerful woman in my view is someone with humility," Beth said, and the "ability to help and set a positive atmosphere for others who are not just in your company, but in your sphere . . . recognizing your impact and the opportunity to help others," she said. "That, to me, is power."[9]

Dear Younger Me,

I have two pieces of advice to share with you:

1. *Always bring your authentic self to all you do. Everyone around you benefits the most when you are 100 percent you.*
2. *Ask for what you want, because no one can read your mind. Confidence and resiliency keep us confident, give us courage, and keep us moving forward.*

CHAPTER SEVENTEEN

Gabby Giffords

FORMER CONGRESSWOMAN AND GUN SAFETY ADVOCATE

Gabby Giffords. PHOTO COURTESY OF GIFFORDS

In 2002, Gabby Giffords became the youngest woman ever elected to the Arizona State Senate. In 2006, she became the third woman in Arizona's history to be elected to the United States Congress. A rising political star, she was elected to a second and then a third term in the House of Representatives.

But on January 8, 2011, her life changed forever.

She was standing in an Arizona supermarket parking lot, excited to be hosting her first "Congress on Your Corner" event with constituents.

"That January morning, I had been looking forward to spending time with the people I represented, talking about hopes and needs," she wrote in the *New York Times*. "It was the part of the job I loved the most."[1]

Suddenly, a gunman ran up to the crowd and opened fire with a 9mm pistol. Intending to assassinate Gabby, he shot her in the head at close range, shattering her skull. He shot eighteen other people as well. Six of them died, and early reports listed Gabby among those killed. The bullet had entered just above her left eye, flying through her brain and out the back of her head. She was rushed to the hospital, where she was listed in critical condition.

Doctors put her in an induced coma so that her swollen brain could rest, increasing her chances of survival. But doctors weren't sure if she would ever come out of the coma. Her brain was swelling so much that part of her skull had to be removed. She couldn't speak because language function is located in the left hemisphere, where the bullet tore through. She was put on a ventilator so she could breathe.

Less than a week later, her eyes began to flutter. When her husband, Mark Kelly, asked if she could hear him, she moved her thumb ever so slightly but unmistakably in a thumbs-up sign. It was the beginning of a remarkable recovery, aided by physical therapy, occupational therapy, music therapy, and speech therapy. She had surgery to replace the part of her skull that had been removed to relieve the pressure from fluid leaking in her brain.

Even though she could barely move the right side of her body and words were a struggle, Gabby was determined to resume her congressional duties.

In 2011, she returned to the House of Representatives and received a standing ovation. But over the next year it became clear that she needed to focus her energy on her recovery. In 2012, she stood on the House floor and announced her resignation in a letter read by her friend and fellow congresswoman Debbie Wasserman Schultz.

"I don't remember much from that terrible day but I have never forgotten my constituents, my colleagues or the millions of Americans with whom I share great hopes for this nation," Gabby wrote. "To all of them, thank you for your prayers, your cards, your well wishes and your support. And even as I have worked to regain my speech, thank you for your faith and my ability to be your voice. . . . From my first steps and first words after being shot to my current physical and speech therapy, I have given all of myself to being able to walk back onto the House floor this year to represent Arizona's Eighth Congressional District. However, today I know that now is not the time. I have more work to do on my recovery before I can again serve in elected office."[2]

Part of her recovery has focused on navigating aphasia, a disorder resulting from brain damage in the area responsible for processing language.

"The words are there in my brain," she said. "I just can't get them out"[3]

In addition to pouring her energy into recovery and raising awareness about aphasia, Gabby and her husband founded GIFFORDS, an organization that works to help prevent gun violence by disrupting the gun lobby's influence on the political system. Although she was no longer serving in Congress, Gabby began actively working to promote gun safety through legislative action.

In 2020, she gave an inspirational speech at the Democratic National Convention, focused on ending gun violence. "I've known the darkest of days. Days of pain and uncertain recovery," she said. "But confronted by despair, I've summoned hope. Confronted by paralysis and aphasia, I responded with grit and determination. I put one foot in front of the other. I found one word and then I found another. My recovery is a daily fight, but fighting makes me stronger. Words once came easily. Today I struggle to speak, but I have not lost my voice."[4]

Gabby's voice promoting gun safety continued to echo through the halls of Capitol Hill, and in 2022, President Joe Biden awarded her the Presidential Medal of Freedom, the nation's highest civilian honor. In presenting the medal, Biden called Gabby "one of the most courageous people I've ever known."[5]

During the awards ceremony, Biden pointed out that he had recently signed the most comprehensive piece of gun safety legislation in decades. He credited Gabby, and others whose lives have been directly impacted by gun violence, for helping to push that bipartisan legislation through.

"She's the embodiment of a single signature American trait: never, ever give up," Biden said during the ceremony.[6]

Gabby's perseverance was the subject of *Gabby Giffords Won't Back Down*, a documentary film released in 2022. It showcased her long road to recovery as well as her advocacy efforts on behalf of gun reform.

Gabby hopes her personal journey can serve as an inspiration to anyone facing adversity. "For me it has been really important to move ahead, to not look back," she said in an interview on *CBS Sunday Morning*. "I hope others are inspired to keep moving forward no matter what." And then she repeated that last line for emphasis: "No matter what."[7]

Dear Younger Me,

A lot has happened to me over the years, much of which no one could have ever seen coming. Who would have guessed that the thing that would equip me best to handle it all would be all the time I spent when I was younger riding my horse, getting thrown off, and having to get back on? But I have a happy, rich life filled with friends and family, and I feel fulfilled because I am making an impact every day. I encourage you to focus on studying, your horses, and your family, and to move ahead! Do not look back! Strong women get things done, and you can do this!

CHAPTER EIGHTEEN

Julia Gillard

LAWYER AND FORMER PRIME MINISTER

Julia Gillard. DILMA ROUSSEFF FROM FLICKR

ON JUNE 24, 2010, JULIA GILLARD WAS SWORN IN AS PRIME minister of Australia—the first female ever to hold that position. Her tenure in office was marked by so much gender discrimination and so many sexist comments that in 2012, she gave a speech that called out sexism and became known all over the world.

The groundbreaking and history-making speech was voted the most unforgettable moment in Australian television history by the *Guardian*. It made headlines across the globe. Julia said the speech struck a chord because she was speaking on behalf of so many women who have silently experienced discrimination themselves.

"I think that speech helps deal with those frustrations and unlock a little sense of power," she told *Forbes* magazine. "It is possible to stand up and name and shame sexism and misogyny."[1]

Julia strongly believes, however, that gender discrimination is not an issue women alone should be responsible for solving, or that should be isolated to a particular effort. Rather, she said, all institutions should continually prioritize equality.

"It's not one day of the year where you have a women's leadership program or some event," she said. "It's core business, every day."[2]

The issue of women's leadership has long been at the top of Julia's agenda. In 2010, she coauthored a book about overcoming inequality called *Women and Leadership: Real Lives, Real Lessons*.

"If you've got a passion to create a better world," Julia said, "then really there's no better way of making that come true than being a leader. . . . Leadership has got its stresses and strains but the impact you can have whether it's in politics, business, law, civil society, news media, technology, is heightened by that leadership platform. You too can make a real difference for the lives of others around you."[3]

As a female leader, Julia was the target of many gender-related attacks by political opponents and the media. But she learned to keep those attacks from getting to her by working on her "own sense of self," shoring up her inner resources, and focusing on her accomplishments.[4]

"I couldn't let myself feel good or bad depending on the headlines," she told *Harvard Business Review*. "I couldn't let it get in my head. I knew that ultimately what would count would be what I achieved during my time in office. It takes discipline and resilience, but I've always believed those are muscles. If you work them, they get stronger."[5]

In 2017, Julia became chair of a nonprofit called Beyond Blue, one of Australia's leading mental health organizations, which focuses awareness and resources on the issues of anxiety, depression, and suicide. Julia's father was a psychiatric nurse, and when she was a young girl, her father helped her recognize the importance of mental health care facilities.

In 2018, she was appointed inaugural chair of the Global Institute for Women's Leadership (GIWL) at King's College in London. Through research and advocacy, GIWL tackles the issues associated with women being underrepresented and undervalued in leadership roles.

A fierce advocate for women's rights, health care, and education, Julia also served as Australia's deputy prime minister, minister for education, minister for employment and workplace relations, and minister for social inclusion. She was also the first female leader of the Australian Labor Party.

Growing up, however, it never occurred to Julia to go into politics.

"I was never the kid who at seven, 10, or 12 said, 'I want to be the prime minister when I grow up,'" Julia said. "That was like saying, 'I want to be an astronaut'—undoable."[6]

But when she went to college, she got involved in a student movement opposing financial cutbacks in education. That ignited the fires of public policy and activism, and Julia took the lead nationally in the movement.

People started asking her to consider stepping into the political arena, and she began to realize "it would be a fantastic way of putting my values into action."[7]

Julia knows as well as anyone that putting your values into action often comes with personal attacks. She advises aspiring leaders to keep working on their sense of self and not let outside opinions, scrutiny, or insults influence anything on the inside.

"It's everything from what we're wearing to the most recent work we have done," she said. "I think it's very important to have a sense of self that is stronger than that. I am still the same Julia Gillard whether the headlines are good or bad."[8]

Dear Younger Me,

To forge a path in any field in life, it is vital to own your sense of purpose and to know what you want your life to be about. It's important to ask: What's driving you? What are your values? What's your vision for your own life?

Then, you should write it out and reach for it on the toughest of days. It is an excellent grounding exercise that has always helped bring my goals sharply into focus.

Use your time preciously. Every day in human history has brought with it the struggle to manage the tension between getting the urgent done and finding time for the important. Find the discipline to consider and do today what will most matter in five, ten, twenty years' time. It will pay dividends.

CHAPTER NINETEEN

Dr. Temple Grandin

AUTISM ADVOCATE AND ANIMAL BEHAVIORIST

Dr. Temple Grandin. PHOTO BY ROSALIE WINARD, COURTESY OF DR. TEMPLE GRANDIN

TEMPLE GRANDIN, PHD, IS A PROFESSOR, ANIMAL BEHAVIOR-ist, inventor, and one of the most highly respected autism experts in the world. She has published more than a dozen books, written more than sixty scientific papers, given hundreds of speeches, and earned multiple degrees.

But when she was a child, doctors told her parents she had brain damage and would need to be institutionalized.

Temple was withdrawn and didn't talk until she was almost four years old. She couldn't stand loud noises and was extremely sensitive to touch. She felt anxious and threatened by everything in her surroundings. She was bullied and teased for being different.

Middle school and high school were the worst, she said. People called her "tape recorder" because of her repetitive speech patterns. She would say the same thing multiple times in a row. "It really hurt," she said.[1]

Temple's mother worked hard to get her daughter the help she needed, seeking out special needs experts and mentors who appreciated Temple's unique mind. They created safe space and brought out Temple's strengths, like visual thinking. Although Temple wasn't diagnosed until later in life, her mother believed early on that Temple had autism.

"My brain is visually indexed," Temple said. "Everything in my mind works like a search engine set for the image function, and you type in a key word and I get pictures."[2]

Autistic children are often labeled as problems because they don't fit into traditional educational models. That was the case with Temple, and she has dedicated her career to bringing attention to different ways children with autism can be redirected to harness their skills and raise their self-esteem. Their fixations, for example, can be applied in positive and productive ways. "I was the goofball that didn't want to study," she said in a 2010 TED Talk called "The World Needs All Kinds of Minds": "Let's say the kid's fixated on Legos, let's get him building. If the kid's fixated on race cars, let's use it for math."[3]

Temple's ability to articulate how her mind operates has led to unprecedented awareness and understanding of the autistic brain. For a long time, many people thought autism was a disease to be cured. And while Temple is forthcoming about the fact that nonverbal autism is more of a challenge, she still advocates for harnessing the unique strengths of autistic minds.

"Rigid academic and social expectations could wind up stifling a mind that, while it might struggle to conjugate a verb, could one day take us to the stars," she said.[4]

While some scientists are researching ways to identify and change autistic genes, Temple points out that many people throughout history who we think of as geniuses actually have high-functioning autism—formerly called Asperger's syndrome.

"If you got rid of all the genes that cause autism, you'd be rid of Carl Sagan, you'd be rid of Mozart. Einstein today would be labeled autistic," she said. "Half of all the people that work at these big tech companies have got at least a mild version of Asperger's. If you didn't have a little bit of those Asperger autistic genes, you wouldn't even have any computers."[5]

One of Temple's priorities is getting autistic people into the workforce, with jobs that value their specific skills of pattern recognition, logic, and attention to detail.

She says she has noticed that many young children growing up in Silicon Valley have internships in the technology industry. "When the kid is maybe 11 years old he's taught programming. By the time the kid is in high school, he's doing mom and dad's work on the computer," Temple said. "Those are the lucky ones."[6]

But then there are people with autism whose families aren't aware that the autistic brain is wired with certain problem-solving strengths. Temple sees many of them when she's doing book signings. "I go out somewhere away from Silicon Valley and I see a guy come up to the book table, he's got a big ponytail, and ought to be going to computer school, and they want to put him on welfare," she said. "I say no, he needs to be going to computer school."[7]

Many of Temple's books serve as guides for tapping into the unique strengths of autistic people and applying those traits in specific social situations, relationships, and careers. She has also written about navigating sensory challenges, which are common among people with autism. Temple's own sensory struggles led to what is perhaps her most famous invention: the squeeze machine. When she was a senior in high school, she visited her aunt's ranch in Arizona, where she saw a chute that held cows in place for vaccination. She realized that the deep pressure from the chute was calming for the cows, and she thought something similar might help relieve her anxiety. So she invented the squeeze machine, also called a hug box, an instrumental stress-relieving device for people with autism. Her scientific paper on the machine and why it worked was published in the *Journal of Child and Adolescent Psychopharmacology*.

Temple's experience with the cows on her aunt's Arizona ranch also led her to realize that people with autism and animals share similar fears, anxieties, and sensitivities. These insights led her to study animal behavior, and she became an animal sciences professor at Colorado State University. She has designed humane livestock handling facilities for all of the major meat companies, and lectures around the world about humane slaughtering methods.

In 2017, Temple was inducted into the National Women's Hall of Fame. Colorado State University president Tony Frank called her "a role model for young women everywhere" who "continues to serve as an advocate for women in the sciences, for young people with autism, and for anyone unwilling to let artificial boundaries stand in the way of their personal and professional success."[8]

Dear Younger Me,

When you get bullied and teased in high school, you should tell yourself that life will get better in the future. Many people who do great things later in life were the kids who had painful experiences inflicted by high school bullies.

CHAPTER TWENTY

Maura Healey

LAWYER AND POLITICIAN

Maura Healey. PHOTO COURTESY OF THE GOVERNOR'S OFFICE

As the newest governor of Massachusetts, Maura Healey has made history many times.

In 2022, she became the first woman ever elected governor of the state of Massachusetts. She also became the first openly lesbian governor-elect of any state in the country.

In her victory speech, she told supporters, "Tonight I want to say something to every little girl and every young LGBTQ person out there. I hope tonight shows you that you can be whatever, whoever you want to be and nothing and no one can ever get in your way except your own imagination and that's not going to happen."[1]

And while Maura sees the historic nature of her victory as a chance to set an example for future leaders, she also points out that it was a long time coming.

"While I'm honored to be the first lesbian governor, I just wish it hadn't taken so long," she said, "and I sure hope that I'm not the last."[2]

Maura prioritizes creating an environment where people feel supported and protected to be who they authentically are. Since her election, young people have written her letters and approached her at events, thanking her for setting an example.

"When you have LGBTQ+ youth three times more likely to miss school because they don't feel safe or three times more likely to commit suicide, it's so important to make sure they feel safe and that somebody has their back," she said.[3]

When Kim Driscoll, formerly the mayor of Salem, Massachusetts, joined Maura in the state capitol, they became the first all-woman team to serve as governor and lieutenant governor. With a long-standing personal and professional passion for civil rights and human rights, Maura takes great pride in paving the way.

"People can't imagine what they can be unless they see somebody doing what they want to do," she said. "Representation really matters, particularly in politics and boardrooms."[4]

In 2007, Maura was hired by Attorney General Martha Coakley, serving as chief of the Civil Rights Division. She made history in that role as well when she spearheaded Massachusetts's challenge to the federal Defense of Marriage Act. It was the country's first successful lawsuit against the 1996 law that allowed states to deny marriage rights to same-sex couples. Maura's case, which went to the United States Supreme Court, ended in victory for same-sex unions across the country.

Human Rights Campaign president Chad Griffin called Maura "one of the staunchest advocates for equality we have in this country."[5]

Maura made history again when she was elected Massachusetts attorney general in 2014, the first openly gay attorney general of any state in the country. She was known as the "People's Lawyer" for taking on some of the nation's most powerful companies and institutions, such as ExxonMobil (for misleading people about climate change) and Purdue Pharma (for misleading people about the addictive nature of opioids).

She also broke what had been known as the "curse of the attorney general" in Massachusetts. Since 1958, six former attorneys general in the state had run for governor. All of them lost.

After her election as governor in 2022, Maura continued to advocate for the underdog. Equal rights and human rights, including immigration reform and advocacy, topped her agenda. Her grandparents had come to the United States from Ireland, which has given her a deeply personal connection to immigration issues.

"I am the granddaughter of immigrants, this is a country of immigrants, it is part of what makes us great as a country" she said in a postelection interview with the Irish news site EchoLive, indicating her intention to focus on immigration reform.[6]

Leading up to the election, Maura's gubernatorial campaign ads became known for highlighting her talent as a basketball player. Her parents divorced when she was young, and her mother sold her wedding ring to afford to pave a basketball court behind their house. Maura went on to cocaptain the women's basketball team at Harvard University, then went overseas to play professional basketball in Austria. She had to go abroad to play professionally because there was no women's basketball league in the United States at the time.

"Now look how far we've come with the WNBA and other professional sports leagues for women," she said. "But we still have work to do."[7]

On the campaign trail, Maura made it a priority to play basketball with young people around the state. The year she was elected, 2022, was the fiftieth anniversary of Title IX, the federal civil rights law that prohibits sex-based discrimination in education.

Maura called Title IX "momentous" and said it "was a huge deal and made so much possible."[8]

She said sports helped her learn about "self-esteem, confidence, resilience and teamwork, and not being afraid. Playing basketball helped a great deal especially when I first ran for office, first got up on a stage, and when I gave my very first speech."[9]

While Maura is proud of her many history-making victories in public office, including her newest role as governor, she sees each of those wins not as isolated victories but as opportunities to continue to advocate for everyone to feel safe being who they are.

"I hope as governor I can make sure that I'm leading the fight against bigotry and discrimination," she said, "so people can live their lives authentically."[10]

Dear Younger Me,

You can always trust yourself, and never be afraid to be yourself. You can achieve anything you put your mind to. See it, believe it, BE it!

CHAPTER TWENTY-ONE

S. E. Hinton

AUTHOR

S. E. Hinton. AP PHOTO/STF

SUSAN ELOISE HINTON IS CREDITED WITH STARTING THE young adult genre. Her wildly successful first novel, *The Outsiders*, has been translated into twenty-three languages, sold millions of copies, and ranks second only to *Charlotte's Web* in terms of total book sales for young readers. Susan began writing her breakout novel when she was just fifteen years old, and that year she got a D in creative writing.

"I didn't do my homework," she told *Good Day Chicago*. "I was writing a book!"[1]

That book came into the world two years later, in 1967, when she was a seventeen-year-old freshman at the University of Tulsa. She hadn't ever intended to publish it, but the mother of one of her friends read the manuscript and had a hunch that it was destined for greatness. The friend's mother happened to know someone who was a children's book writer, so Susan got the name of the writer's agent, and sent off the manuscript. Viking Press scooped it up but suggested she use her initials, S. E. Hinton, so that male reviewers and critics would take the book more seriously.

Her first royalty check was for ten dollars, and *The Outsiders* almost went out of print as an adult book. But teachers all over the country began using it in their classrooms. So it was rebranded and marketed as a young adult (YA) book. Up until that time, stories in the YA genre consisted primarily of prom queen sagas, high school crushes, sports, and homecoming dances. *The Outsiders* changed all that with its gritty, realistic portrayal of teen angst, social-class warfare, and gang violence.

Although the book is fiction, it's based on Susan's personal experience at Will Rogers High School in Tulsa, Oklahoma, where students were divided into two groups: one blue-collar, the other upper-class. Those two groups are the Greasers and the Socs (pronounced SO-shes), the rival gangs in *The Outsid-*

ers. In real life, Susan was a Greaser. One of her good friends got beaten up by a Soc on the way home from school, and she wrote a short story about it to process her feelings.

"I wrote it because I was mad at the social situation," she said, "everybody getting into their little groups and staying in their little groups and not having friends outside their groups, so I took this to extremes to write about the Greasers and the Socs. When I was in high school I saw a lot of rough things going on. There was none of this in the literature at that time."[2]

Even if young readers can't relate to gang violence, Susan said, they can relate to the fear, sadness, and angst of being a teenager. They can also relate to feeling like an outsider.

"There's a lot of universal connections to be made," she told the Oklahoma Historical Society.[3]

Susan started writing as soon as she could read. She was a voracious reader as a child, and soon ran out of books in the library that appealed to her. So she began writing stories of her own. She also used writing as a solace during her abusive childhood. She kept telling herself things would get better, all the while honing her ability to craft honest, authentic stories brimming with raw emotion.

But writing didn't always come easily. The success of *The Outsiders* led to so much pressure to produce another book, Susan found herself struggling with severe writer's block that lasted four years.

"I had places where I couldn't think of anything to say, didn't want to say anything, didn't feel like writing," she said in an interview celebrating the forty-fifth anniversary of *The Outsiders*.[4]

But she plowed through it, eventually writing at least two pages each day, which resulted in her second book, *That Was Then, This Is Now*, a young adult novel about foster brothers who drift apart. Two more novels—*Rumble Fish* and *Tex*—followed. All have been made into feature films.

The Outsiders movie, released in 1983 and directed by the renowned Francis Ford Coppola, came about because high schoolers in California loved the book so much they sent a petition to Coppola asking him to make it into a movie. Not only did he say yes, he also brought Susan on to help write the screenplay and gave her a director's chair on the movie set. It turns out he wanted the movie to be more like the book than she did.

Susan said she would cut certain parts from the screenplay, and "he'd read it and say, 'But this sentence isn't like the one in the book,' and I would say, 'No Francis, it's better,' and he'd say, 'No, we're making this for the audience, and they want it just like the book.' . . . . So that was my big problem working with him; he wanted it just like the book!"[5]

The movie featured actors who are now household names but at the time were just beginning their careers, including Tom Cruise, Matt Dillon, Emilio Estevez, Diane Lane, and Patrick Swayze.

In a peek behind the scenes, Susan shared a story about one day on the set when Cruise told her he'd eaten too much at lunch and didn't think he'd be able to make it through a fight scene that was coming up that afternoon. She said, "'Well Tom, would you feel better if you threw up?' And he said, 'You know, I think I would.' So I took him over to the catering truck and made him drink raw eggs until he threw up. And then he felt much better and did the stunt perfectly. . . . We all knew he was going to be a star."[6]

Susan remains in close contact with all the actors. "I knew them when they were kids," she said, "and not when they were stars."[7]

In 1988, Susan received the first-ever Margaret A. Edwards Award from the Young Adult Services Division of the American Library Association for her contribution to teen literature. Ten years later, she was inducted into the Oklahoma Writers Hall of Fame.

She doesn't take for granted the success or the timelessness of her books, especially *The Outsiders*, which continues to resonate with young readers whose parents and even grandparents enjoyed it when they were young.

"It's just been amazing to me how this book keeps speaking to each new generation," she said. "Now parents are giving their children the book and saying, 'I really liked this when I was a kid; I'll bet you will too.'"[8]

Dear Younger Me,

I am so proud of you, knowing what you wanted to do at a young age, practicing constantly for it by both reading and writing, working hard while others were goofing around—I owe you!

CHAPTER TWENTY-TWO

Janice Bryant Howroyd

ENTREPRENEUR

Janice Bryant Howroyd. COURTESY OF JANICE BRYANT HOWROYD

Janice Bryant Howroyd is the first Black woman ever to run a billion-dollar business. *Forbes* magazine listed her among the nation's wealthiest self-made women. She's the founder and CEO of the ActOne Group, a business solutions company with more than seventeen thousand clients.

But in the 1970s, she moved to Los Angeles with just a few hundred dollars, a tiny office, and a dream of starting her own company.

Now that company has twenty-six hundred employees around the world. In its main branch hangs a painting inspired by a landmark civil rights case, *Brown v. Board of Education*, which ended decades of legal racial segregation in public education. In 1954, the U.S. Supreme Court struck down as unconstitutional state laws that established separate schools for students of different races.

"I'm a product of that energy," Janice told the *Los Angeles Times*.[1]

In fact, in addition to being a renowned entrepreneur, Janice is known for being one of the first students to desegregate her local North Carolina school. In the 1960s, she was one of the first Black students ever to attend an all-white high school. Her decision was an act of courage that sprang from discrimination and personal hardship. On the first day of school, Janice's teacher denounced affirmative action policies and told the class that Black Americans were well suited to be slaves.

In a second incident, a boy stood up in history class and gave a racist speech. Janice went home crying and told her parents she didn't want to go back to that school. Her father gave her the option of transferring to the all-Black high school in their community.

But Janice made the choice to go back. She held her head high. She wanted to prove everyone wrong by becoming successful. And that's exactly what she did. Janice won a full scholarship to North Carolina State Agricultural and Technical College.

After graduation, she went to Los Angeles to visit her sister, who was married to an executive at *Billboard* magazine. He got Janice a job doing clerical work and discovered that she had a knack for recruiting employees. In 1978, with some money she had saved up and a $533 loan from her brother and mother, she decided to start her own employment agency. She had a tiny office, a landline, and a telephone book.

She also had a passion for empowering people to succeed.

"The first time I felt empowered, it changed my life," she said, "because I saw what was possible when people feel in control of their own lives."[2]

That first feeling of empowerment came when Janice was a little girl, giving a speech during an Easter service at her family's church.

"Stepping out to center stage on one of the most attended days of the year, my heart pounded and my palms were slick with sweat," she said. "Between the time I walked toward the stage and the first words I uttered, my mother had miraculously moved from the backstage to take a center seat in the front row."[3]

And then, a few words into her speech, Janice paused. "I looked into the audience and saw her with her powder blue hat and dress. She looked up at me, she smiled, and I knew I had an anchor," Janice said. "With her one smile, I moved from panic to power."[4]

That power translated into an Easter speech that wowed the entire congregation. "They weren't just listening to what I was saying; they were feeling what I was saying," Janice remembered. "Their reactions empowered me further."[5]

Janice never forgot that feeling. She credits it with contributing to her confidence and self-trust later in life. In the 1980s, when companies started laying off workers in large numbers, she pivoted her business to help employers find temporary employees to fill the gaps. Her client list grew larger and larger. She became so successful that she expanded the temp component of her agency into four major areas: clerical, engineering, entertainment, and technology.

Out of the technology area came the launch of a high-tech division that was ahead of its time. It sprang from Janice's charity work. She was helping to sponsor a low-income high school when she noticed that the students didn't have the computer skills they needed to be successful in the workforce after graduation. Realizing the need for tech-savvy employees prompted her to launch the high-tech recruiting arm of her company, which has grown exponentially.

Over the years, Janice's philanthropic work has included mentoring female entrepreneurs looking to launch and expand their businesses. When Janice was just starting out, the American Women's Economic Development Management Program helped her, so she decided to give back by sponsoring other female entrepreneurs through the same nonprofit organization. Janice has also given college scholarships to low-income and minority students. And she helped organize and sponsor the Minority Business Opportunity Day Trade Fair, an annual event in Los Angeles.

In 2016, President Barack Obama appointed Janice to the President's Board of Advisors on Historically Black Colleges and Universities. She has also served as a member of the Women's Leadership Board at Harvard University's Kennedy School of Government.

Whether she's doing charity work, helping new entrepreneurs, conducting business, or a combination of these, she operates using her signature "elements of empowerment for

114

leadership" and encourages businesses to incorporate them. The elements include clearly defining goals, offering support, emphasizing teamwork, providing meaning, giving workers the tools to be successful on their own, and letting employees know they are valued.

Looking back, Janice sees how feeling valued helped her overcome anxiety, harness her courage, and deliver that Easter speech so many years ago. "I knew my speech was a critical part of the Easter production, which motivated me to give my best effort," Janice said. "Employees operate with a similar mindset."[6]

A key aspect of empowering people to succeed, Janice believes, is a constant examination and recalibration of systems in the workplace that might be unwittingly holding people back from feeling confident.

"Like so many women," she said, "I've tended to look inward to learn what's wrong with me first versus examining the role of others or looking for systemic failures."[7]

And while looking inward is important, Janice said, so is looking outward at the organization.

"Today, I don't doubt myself so quickly," she said. "If I'm not feeling empowered, it might be because the system around me is lacking the essential elements of empowerment. If my employees don't feel empowered, it's not necessarily their fault. It's my job to examine our organization and ensure the foundation is in place for them to feel confident and in control. I know from experience that this effort is worthwhile."[8]

Dear Younger Me,

Please never compromise who you are personally to become who you wish to be professionally.

CHAPTER TWENTY-THREE
Dr. Laurie Marker
ZOOLOGIST AND
CONSERVATION BIOLOGIST

Dr. Laurie Marker. COURTESY OF CHEETAH CONSERVATION FUND

CHEETAHS ARE DISAPPEARING. NINETY PERCENT OF THEM have died. There are fewer than ten thousand of them left on the planet. And Laurie Marker, PhD, the world's foremost cheetah expert, says if we can bring them back from the brink of extinction, we can learn how to save other species and entire ecosystems as well.

In other words, "save the cheetah, change the world," according to Laurie. "If we can get the cheetahs right, then we can begin to save other species."[1]

She has made it her mission to do just that.

"We always think there is someone else who will do something, that 'they' will take care of it," she said. "I realized early in my work that there is no 'they,' and so I decided that I would take action to save the cheetah from extinction."[2]

Although Laurie grew up surrounded by animals—she learned how to care for dogs, cats, rabbits and goats as a child and got her first horse at age four—her work with cheetahs all began with a billboard.

In 1974, she moved from California to Oregon to open a winery. But it wasn't paying the bills. While she was out driving one day, she spotted a billboard for a new animal park called Wildlife Safari. The billboard featured a cheetah. Intrigued, she took a job there to make ends meet. It was one of the only places in the world with cheetahs, and from her first moment in their presence, Laurie was captivated. She was also concerned, because she learned that cheetahs survive only around five years in captivity.

She began speaking to scientists around the world, but no one seemed to know much about them. So, with the ten cheetahs at Wildlife Safari as her subjects, she poured herself into studying their behavior and biology. Based on her research,

Laurie eventually developed the country's most successful cheetah breeding program.

"The next thing I knew, I found out I was the expert on cheetahs in the world,"[3] she said during a TEDx Talk titled "What If We Lost the Cheetah?"

In 1977, Laurie travelled to Namibia, a country in southern Africa that has the world's largest population of cheetahs. She brought Khayam, a cheetah she had raised in captivity. She wanted to see if she could teach Khayam how to hunt in the wild.

But when she arrived in Namibia, she was shocked. "Nothing that I had experienced prepared me for what I saw," she said.[4] Farmers in Namibia were trapping, shooting, and killing hundreds of cheetahs each year. In the 1980s alone, they killed nearly ten thousand cheetahs—half of Namibia's cheetah population.

Laurie was determined to find out why. In 1990, after earning her PhD in zoology from Oxford University, she sold all her possessions, moved to Namibia, and started the Cheetah Conservation Fund (CCF) in a small farmhouse.

In talking to the farmers who were killing the cheetahs, she realized that many of them were living on the edge of poverty, and they were only trying to protect their livestock from being hunted.

"Many farmers were poor, and even losing one sheep meant disaster for their families' livelihood," she said. "I had to come up with some real solutions to their problems if they were going to help me save the cheetah."[5]

One of those solutions has been the Livestock Guardian Dog Program, which pairs farmers with specially bred guard dogs to keep wolves, cheetahs, and other native predators away from their livestock. The program has been wildly successful, decreasing predation by nearly 100 percent. It has also helped keep the farmers' children in school, since they used to have to miss classes to herd livestock. Laurie has also taught the farmers how to increase their income and support the local economy by setting up creameries to produce goat milk and cheese.

Today, the CCF has grown into a world-renowned cheetah rehabilitation sanctuary as well as a conservation, research, and education center. The facility houses a cheetah museum, a genetics laboratory, and a veterinary clinic. Laurie has worked with the Smithsonian Institution and the National Cancer Institute on genetics research, including mapping the cheetah genome. Part of her mission has also been stopping the illegal poaching and trafficking of cheetahs.

Laurie's life's work demonstrates what can happen as a result of finding and following a passion.

"I didn't start out to become who I am today," she said. "I met a cheetah and it changed my life. . . . Falling in love with a cheetah gave me a mission."[6]

Her inspiration for all that she has accomplished has been, unsurprisingly, the very animal she has worked so hard to protect.

A cheetah's eyes zero in on its target "with laser focus," she said. "Nothing else matters. And that's what's made the cheetah a successful predator. And it's that kind of focus that's allowed me to do exactly what I've done. . . . What I've learned is that you can do the most extraordinary things if you're willing to pursue your objective with that kind of focus and determination. Just like a cheetah."[7]

Dear Younger Me,

Everything takes time. When it feels like everyone and everything is against moving things forward or blocking your way, don't be discouraged. Negotiate your way through the maze and don't take no for an answer. Don't be afraid to ask for what you need. Speak up. Be bold. Keep focused.

CHAPTER TWENTY-FOUR

Midori

VIOLINIST

Midori. PHOTO BY NIGEL PARRY, 2022, COURTESY OF
KIRSHBAUM ASSOCIATES

AS THE CHILD OF A PROFESSIONAL VIOLINIST IN JAPAN, Midori Goto would tag along during her mother's rehearsals, often taking naps in the auditorium. Two days after one such rehearsal, Midori began humming the entire Bach concerto the orchestra had been practicing.

She was two years old.

From that point on, Midori's love for music could not be contained. No longer content to just memorize melodies from the symphony, she began climbing up on the family's piano in an attempt to reach the violin her mother kept there. When Midori turned three, her mother gave her a special gift: a 1/16-size violin of her own, along with lessons.

At age six, Midori gave her first public performance in her native Japan, setting the stage for her recognition as a worldwide child prodigy. Several years later, she and her mother moved to New York. After years of enduring an unhappy arranged marriage, Midori's mother decided it was time to start a new life in the United States with her daughter.

They had no money and couldn't speak English, Midori told the *Los Angeles Times*: "It took amazing conviction to come alone to a foreign country with a little kid, and to go against the family wishes. I like to think I have some of that strong-mindedness."[1]

When they arrived in the United States, Midori started violin classes at the famed Juilliard School of Music. For her audition, she played Bach's Chaconne—thirteen minutes long and widely considered one of the most difficult solo violin pieces to master. That same year, she debuted with the New York Philharmonic. She was just eleven years old.

In what would become a legendary performance, as a teenager Midori took to the stage with the Boston Symphony Orchestra at the music venue Tanglewood in Lenox, Massachusetts. She performed *Serenade*, by acclaimed musician Leonard Bernstein, in a concert conducted by Bernstein himself. During the performance, one of her violin strings broke. Without missing a beat, she walked up to the concertmaster, borrowed his much bigger violin, and continued playing—until another string broke. This time she borrowed the associate concertmaster's violin. She finished her performance to a standing ovation.

The next morning, a front-page *New York Times* headline read: "Girl, 14, Conquers Tanglewood with 3 Violins."

Midori went on to record her first album at age seventeen and made her critically acclaimed Carnegie Hall debut at age eighteen. As her star continued to rise, Midori used her talents to bring music to children who wouldn't otherwise have access to the arts. After learning that schools were being forced to cut their music education budgets, she created the nonprofit organization Midori and Friends to teach classical music to underserved students in New York City.

Her nonprofit work eventually branched out to other states, and other countries, including her native Japan. Midori's work includes music education programs for students in schools, after-school programs, and hospitals. It also includes music classes for the disabled.

But even as she was bringing the healing power of music to others, Midori was facing her own internal struggles.

In her twenties, she spent time in the hospital after canceling concerts and stepping out of the public eye. She was diagnosed with anorexia and depression. She wrote about this difficult period of her life in her 2004 memoir.

Because of her challenges, she considered becoming a child psychologist. Instead, she returned to the stage while getting a bachelor's and then a master's degree in psychology from New York University. She wrote her master's thesis on the topic of pain.

She also became a much-loved music professor at multiple colleges and was named a United Nations Messenger of Peace for her humanitarian work.

In 2012, Midori was awarded an Honorary Doctorate of Music from Yale University for her "supreme talent" and "commitment to education and community wellbeing."

Upon receiving the award, Midori said, "I started out playing music because of the joy it brings to our lives, but in my work I am also discovering every day the power music has to heal, to educate, to stimulate the human mind in multiple dimensions."[2]

She put this into practice during the COVID pandemic, offering free virtual violin classes to children as a way to bring people together.

As she was making these meaningful connections through music, Midori received one of the highest awards an artist can earn in this country, becoming a Kennedy Center Honoree for lifetime artistic achievement.

Upon accepting the award in 2021, Midori spoke of her hope that the universal language of music could help the world find its way back from the isolation and disconnection that so many people experienced during the pandemic. Together, she said, the opportunities for healing, bonding, and creativity that music provides have the power to help the world "reach toward renewed expression of the dreams and hopes that unify us all."[3]

Dear Younger Me,

The world is in constant change. Respect the past, cherish the present. Invest in the future in a spirit of hopefulness. Embrace and honor what you have and are given; be open to all possible challenges and discoveries. This means that the most meaningful things are those that are closest to your heart. Explore those, while staying grounded. Live in the moment; work and plan for the future. Focus on your learning and you will find joy in the efforts you invested.

CHAPTER TWENTY-FIVE

Julia Parsons

WORLD WAR II CODEBREAKER

Julia Parsons. COURTESY OF JULIA PARSONS

GROWING UP IN THE 1920S AND 1930S, JULIA PARSONS WAS acutely aware of what girls were not allowed to do. She really wanted to play baseball, for example, and climb trees.

But when it came to baseball, girls had to sit on the sidelines.

"All girls could do was cheer for the boys who got to play," she said. "It was upsetting. It was something I wanted to try, but there was nothing I could do about it."[1]

And when she would try to sneak in a climb? "My mother would say, 'Get out of that tree; girls don't climb trees.' But it was something I always wanted to do."

At Christmas, she was given pots and pans, while the boys got Erector Sets and other building toys. "They had something to put together," she said. "I would have loved that. Those were way better presents than pots and pans."

As she grew older, she discovered there were middle school and high school classes that girls weren't allowed to take. "I would have loved to take wood shop and some of those other interesting classes with tools and measurements that boys talked about and that I was drawn to," she said. "It didn't seem fair, and I always felt I could do more if given the chance, but back then girls were just supposed to accept that boys and men had all the advantages and opportunities."

Still, at a time when "college was mostly for boys," Julia managed to graduate from Carnegie Institute of Technology in Pennsylvania, one of the nation's premier technical universities. She wanted to follow her passion for math and engineering, but women weren't allowed to take those classes. When she told people she dreamed of being an engineer, "they laughed and laughed at me," she recalled. "Girls took secretarial courses. Only men were engineers."

But everything changed the summer after she graduated.

It was 1942, and World War II was heating up. Women weren't allowed to serve in combat, but their work options suddenly expanded because so many men were needed on the front lines. President Franklin Roosevelt signed a new law that paved the way for women to join the U.S. Navy in more technical roles. Julia found herself finally able to take courses like math, mechanical drawing, and engineering as part of the WAVES program—Women Accepted for Volunteer Emergency Service.

Even though her father was traditional (he wouldn't let her mother become a nurse, since women were "supposed" to stay home), Julia said he felt immense pride in having a daughter in the military. "I remember him saying, 'Now we can get a flag for the window!'" He hung out a blue star service flag, proud to show passers-by that he had a daughter serving in wartime.

Little did anyone know that Julia's wartime service was about to take an even more exciting turn.

Her training included code-breaking and identifying ships by their silhouettes. She scored so high on all of her exams that she was chosen to be part of an elite group going to the Naval Communications Annex in Washington, DC. As she waited to find out her assignment, an officer came into the room and asked if anyone spoke German. Julia had taken two years of German in high school, so she raised her hand and was whisked off to a top-secret section of WAVES. She immediately began learning how to decode secret messages Nazi radio operators were sending to their submarines.

When it came to decoding these transmissions, every second counted. The German subs, called U-boats, were planting underwater mines and attacking U.S. convoys. Any delay in cracking the codes could mean the difference between life and death for American troops at sea.

Once the women had cracked the codes, American officers would know the locations of the U-boats, and would be able to sink the subs before they could do any further damage. "If we broke the code for that day, it was so exciting," Julia said.

But the excitement was often tempered by the personal nature of the messages the codebreakers were intercepting. One message congratulated a German officer on the birth of his son. Once the code was cracked, the Allies learned the position of that sub and sank it.

"That baby would never see his father," Julia said. "I felt really bad. I understand we needed to sink the subs; I just wish we could have saved more of the crews."

Given the highly classified nature of their work, the women in the WAVES program couldn't tell anyone what they were doing—including their families. If they did divulge the secret, they faced the death penalty.

More than half a century after the war, Julia was touring the National Cryptologic Museum in Maryland. She couldn't believe her eyes. Right there out in the open, on display, were the code-breaking machines, with detailed explanations of how they worked. Julia asked a tour guide: "How can you do this? Our work was a secret!"

The tour guide told her that code-breaking had been declassified thirty years earlier. She never knew. So she began telling her family.

"It's been good to break the silence," she said. Although she does wish she could have told her father before he passed away. "It's sad," she said. "I never got to tell him. He would have been fascinated. And very proud."

Dear Younger Me,

I'm proud of you. But try to be more understanding. Have more compassion. Do more things to help other people. And try to appreciate your parents while they are still living.

CHAPTER TWENTY-SIX

Nancy Pelosi

FORMER SPEAKER OF THE HOUSE

Nancy Pelosi. AUTHOR JOHN HARRINGTON; OFFICIAL GOVERN-
MENT PHOTO

As the first female Democratic leader of the U.S. House of Representatives and the first woman ever to serve as Speaker of the House, Nancy Pelosi has spent her entire political career breaking gender barriers: "breaking the marble ceiling," as she says.[1]

But she never even intended to run for office. In fact, she was raised to believe that women were supposed to stay out of the government spotlight and that their primary role in politics was to help men get elected to positions of power and influence.

Her father was a U.S. congressman who later became Baltimore's first Italian American mayor. She grew up watching and helping her mother, whose name was also Nancy, support his political career from behind the scenes. As the youngest of six children and the only daughter, "little Nancy," as she was called, was on hand as her mother organized volunteers and welcomed constituents into their home to hear their stories, answer their questions, and help them find services.

While her father was at the U.S. Capitol, and later Baltimore city hall, it was her mother who served as the "unofficial" public servant, Nancy said.[2]

She grew up understanding that the place for women's personal and professional ambitions was in the back seat. Her mother had wanted to become a lawyer but was forced to drop out of law school when three of her sons were sick at the same time with whooping cough. So instead, "big Nancy" focused on furthering her husband's career.

But little Nancy always felt the stirring of something more. When her mother asked whether she might like to become a nun, Nancy remembers thinking she would actually rather become a priest. "It seemed like there was more power there," she recalled.[3]

In high school, Nancy experienced what she would later describe as an "encounter with history," when her mother bowed out of a special dinner so her daughter could take her place at the head table.[4] The guest of honor was John F. Kennedy, who would become president of the United States just a few years later. As a college student, Nancy attended his inauguration. She remembers being inspired by his leadership during the years that followed, calling his public service "not just a memory, but a living force that still asks every citizen to lead—and perhaps that is the most precious gift of all."[5]

Nancy took that inspiration with her over the years that followed, as she got married, moved to San Francisco, and started a family. She became more active in running political campaigns. But she still didn't consider running for office herself. Instead, she followed in her own mother's footsteps, working tirelessly behind the scenes in California to support male candidates.

And then, in 1987, that all changed. A dear friend, who was also a U.S. congresswoman, called Nancy to her bedside. Her name was Sala Burton, and she was dying of cancer. There was going to be a special election to fill her seat in the House of Representatives, and she wanted Nancy to run for that seat. She knew Nancy would stand up for the underdog and fight for equal rights. It took some convincing. Nancy was shocked that Burton was even asking. She had never imagined herself as a political candidate.

"When Sala Burton came along," Nancy recalled, "here was a woman, a member of Congress, making a decision about who she wanted to succeed her. That hardly ever happens. Men usually make the decisions."[6]

But, encouraged by the faith her friend was placing in her, Nancy finally said yes. Her campaign slogan was: "A voice that will be heard."

And she was. After a hard-fought campaign, Nancy won a seat in the U.S. House of Representatives. The mother of five rose up the ranks, becoming the first woman ever to lead a political party in Congress and eventually serving four terms as Speaker.

Women's rights have always topped her political agenda, as have human rights, environmental protection, gun control, affordable housing, and affordable healthcare. One of her proudest accomplishments came in 2010, when she helped President Barack Obama write the Affordable Care Act and made sure she had the congressional votes to pass it. She said affordable healthcare, along with affordable childcare and housing, are key issues in addressing her priority: children. She cited as her primary motivator the statistic that one out of every five children grows up in poverty.

She is particularly passionate about setting an example for young people everywhere, especially young women, that anything is possible.

Dear Younger Me,

Be yourself. No matter where life takes you, and no matter what happens. It's nice to have mentors and people you admire, but authentically, you are you. Don't forget that. Make contributions that only you can make to the world. If you have an opportunity, no one can undertake it the way you can. And be ready; you never know what's around the next corner!

CHAPTER TWENTY-SEVEN

Kaitlin Roig-DeBellis

EDUCATOR

Kaitlin Roig-DeBellis. PHOTO BY L'ORÉAL, COURTESY OF
KAITLIN ROIG-DEBELLIS

ON DECEMBER 14, 2012, KAITLIN ROIG-DEBELLIS WAS CERtain she was going to die.

She and her first grade students at Sandy Hook Elementary School in Newtown, Connecticut, had just wrapped up their morning meeting when gunshots echoed through the hallway, followed by the sound of shattered glass. Kaitlin knew if they stayed in the classroom, they wouldn't make it out alive.

But there was nowhere to run. The windows were too small to climb out of. The only option was a three-by-four-foot bathroom. She whisked all fifteen students inside it, putting one student on top of the toilet paper holder and several on top of the toilet so they could all fit inside the tiny space.

"I remember so vividly standing there shaking," she recalled, "sure we were living on seconds, maybe minutes. Sure they were our last."[1]

In those harrowing forty-five minutes, Kaitlin said, three things went through her mind.

The first was: "Life. How desperately I wanted this life. The finite and miniscule existence we each have. It goes by way too fast. It is a supreme gift."

The second was: "Loved ones (especially my fiancé in that moment, six months before we were to be married). Our loved ones are the only 'stuff' that matters. Family, friends, the ones who come and stay forever. We must love them fiercely. Tell them. Give them our time."

And time, she said, was the third thing that went through her mind as she and her students huddled in the bathroom praying together for their lives: "Having time is all that really matters. It is fleeting. Celebrate the moments. The big ones, the tiny ones. Every single one. We so often forget that being free to choose how we spend our time is the greatest gift in and of itself. Choose wisely."

After what felt like hours, someone knocked on the classroom door. Kaitlin thought for sure it was the shooter. It turned out to be a police officer. Kaitlin and her fifteen students ran out of the building, having survived one of the nation's deadliest school shootings. Gunman Adam Lanza had killed twenty children and six staff members before turning the gun on himself. Before he left home that day, he also killed his mother.

When Kaitlin and her students eventually came back to their new school—a refurbished building in a neighboring town—they were inundated with gifts from classrooms across the world. Students, parents, and teachers sent them stuffed animals, school supplies, toys, and books. When she saw how touched her students were, she began talking to them about the concept of paying kindness forward. Her class started sending gifts and school supplies to classrooms in need. She saw how excited her students were to be giving to others. She saw that it was helping them heal. It was helping her heal as well.

Barely three weeks after they hid in that tiny bathroom, her students were expressing joy at the prospect of giving to kids in need. She noticed they seemed to be even happier about giving than they were about receiving. Seeing an opportunity to expand this dynamic beyond her school, she created Classes4Classes, a nonprofit social networking program that connects classrooms in need with classrooms that have the resources to help fund things like school supplies and money for field trips. Beyond the exchange of goods, Kaitlin says, the program emphasizes compassion, empathy, and the fact that we're all connected.

But even as her students were giving and receiving gifts, they were understandably still grieving, in shock, and terrified that they could experience another tragedy—especially because they knew hiding in the bathroom had saved their lives, and their new classroom had no bathroom. So Kaitlin asked the school administration for safety measures, including security cameras and a rope ladder to hang out the window in case they needed to escape. When the school denied her requests, she took a leave of absence from teaching and eventually resigned, focusing full time on expanding Classes4Classes.

The year after the shooting, Kaitlin was honored alongside Nobel Prize nominee Malala Yousafzai and shooting survivor Representative Gabby Giffords as one of *Glamour* magazine's Women of the Year.

That same year she received the Dedicated Teacher Award from the Chicago International Conference on Education. She went on to write a book about coping with tragedy, *Choosing Hope: Moving Forward from Life's Darkest Hours.* She travels the world speaking about the impact of that terrifying day and the importance of empathy and hope.

Kaitlin said she frequently speaks to her young daughter about the importance of being brave. But bravery, she emphasizes, isn't the absence of fear. It's about "acting in the face of fear." It's about moving forward when you feel like you can't.

"Worry and anxiety are normal, "she said. "Lean into them. We as a society do a terrible job. We say flippant things like, 'Don't worry, it's fine, you're just making a big deal.' But people and feelings need to be seen. . . . I pray that I can instill in my daughter that even when she is afraid, to do it anyway, because on the other side of that fear is where the magic happens."

Dear Younger Me,

Enjoy the journey. It's not about each high, low, best, worst, happy, sad, big, small moment in our lives. It's about the compilation of all of these; the fabric woven that, when you look back, ultimately becomes your journey. THAT is what makes you, you. Enjoy yours.

CHAPTER TWENTY-EIGHT

Buffy Sainte-Marie

MUSICIAN AND ACTIVIST

Buffy Sainte-Marie. PHOTO BY MATT BARNES

WHEN SHE WAS JUST A TODDLER, BUFFY SAINTE-MARIE WAS taken from her family in the Piapot First Nation in Saskatchewan, Canada, and adopted by a white family in Massachusetts. It was not uncommon at the time for child welfare service workers to take Indigenous children from their biological families, a practice that would later become known as the "Sixties Scoop."

The goal was to erase any trace of Indigenous language, culture, and life.

But Buffy's connection to her roots was too strong to ever be erased. Her heritage coursed through her veins, even when people refused to believe what she knew in her heart to be true.

"Teachers told me that I couldn't possibly be Indigenous," she said. "[I] must be mistaken about that, because the Indians were all gone, a thing of past history."[1]

Buffy has spent her career proving them wrong. Through her music and her social activism, she has pulled back the curtain on various practices throughout history that have caused severe suffering and harm to Indigenous people.

In the 1960s, she recorded "Now That the Buffalo's Gone," a song that drew attention to the practice of forcing Indigenous people off their land. She wrote it after hundreds of Indigenous families in New York and Pennsylvania were kicked out of their homes after a dam was constructed where they lived. The title refers to the bison that provided food and clothing for Indigenous Americans. The bison nearly became extinct in the 1800s, after the US government killed them to drive the Indigenous people onto reservations.

In addition to recording songs about the plight of Indigenous people, Buffy also made music to draw attention to other issues she felt weren't getting the attention they deserved. After seeing wounded soldiers returning home from Vietnam, she wrote and recorded "Universal Soldier" to protest the war. The year was 1963, and the U.S. government was denying any involvement in the Vietnam War.

The same year she recorded "Universal Soldier," she had a respiratory infection and was prescribed what she believed was a course of antibiotics. Unbeknownst to her, they were actually opioids, and she became addicted. After going through the agony of withdrawal, Buffy wrote the song "Cod'ine" in an effort to bring the taboo subject of opioid addiction into the light. Both "Now That the Buffalo's Gone" and "Cod'ine" were released on her 1964 debut album *It's My Way*.

The fact that her music dealt with controversial political subjects got her blacklisted in the 1960s and 1970s by the administrations of Lyndon Johnson and Richard Nixon. She didn't find out about this until two decades later, when a radio station employee showed her a letter on White House stationery that thanked him for refusing to play her music. And although it impacted her career, she came back in force.

In 1983, Buffy became the first Indigenous American to win an Oscar. She won the Academy Award in the Best Original Song category for cowriting "Up Where We Belong" for the film *An Officer and a Gentleman*. The song also earned her the Golden Globe Award.

Although Buffy felt drawn to music from an early age, she was repeatedly shut out of musical opportunities as a child. "When I was in school, I could play music naturally by ear, without lessons," she said. "Anything I heard on the radio, I could play it just by listening. But I was shunned and shamed in school music class, got poor grades, wasn't allowed to be in band or chorus, and told I couldn't be a musician, because I couldn't read European notation."[2]

But while Buffy spent much of her childhood feeling excluded, she has spent a large part of her adulthood making sure Indigenous kids grow up feeling empowered. In the 1980s, when her son Cody was in fifth grade, his teacher asked Buffy to do a unit on Indigenous Americans. Over the course of the next several years, Buffy developed an original curriculum for teaching core subjects through Indigenous points of view. Her effort became a worldwide initiative called the Cradleboard Teaching Project, which connected Indigenous and non-Indigenous students, teachers, and classrooms for fifteen years.

From 1975 to 1981, she also brought Indigenous representation to children and families worldwide as part of the cast of *Sesame Street*. In one of her best-known episodes, she nursed her son Cody and explained to Big Bird what she was doing. It was the first time anyone had breastfed on television.

"See? He's drinking milk from my breast," she told Big Bird during the episode. Big Bird replied, "That's a funny way to feed a baby."

"Lots of mothers feed their babies this way," Buffy said. "Not all mothers, but lots of mothers do."[3]

Later, Buffy looked back on the day she gave birth to Cody in the hospital and recalled a big basket of gifts from a formula company. She told the doctors she wanted to breastfeed, but "the doctors didn't understand about breastfeeding; they had not learned it. The formula companies were putting a lot of money into education in medical hospitals," she said. "There's no money involved in breastfeeding. It's free, therefore there's nobody making a fortune on it."[4]

Buffy continued to make history and break barriers. In 1991, sixteen years after releasing her last album, she became the first person to release a record over the internet.

In 2020, she released her first children's book, *Hey Little Rockabye*, a lullaby about pet adoption. Buffy donated part of the proceeds to the Humane Society of Canada. In the book, a little girl rescues a puppy from a shelter. And Buffy yet again uses her lyrics to convey a meaningful message—this time about love, acceptance, and "caring for all Earth's creatures."[5]

Dear Younger Me,

Sometimes grown-ups are wrong and kids are right.

CHAPTER TWENTY-NINE

Sheryl Sandberg

BUSINESS EXECUTIVE AND PHILANTHROPIST

Sheryl Sandberg. COURTESY OF SANDBERG GOLDBERG BERNTHAL FAMILY FOUNDATION

Sheryl Sandberg is one of the most powerful women in business. She rose to the top of the male-dominated Silicon Valley, where she became chief operating officer of Facebook and was instrumental in building it into one of the world's most profitable and influential companies. In 2012, she became the first woman to serve on Facebook's board of directors. That same year, she was named one of *Time* magazine's 100 Most Influential People in the World.

And she wants more women to join her at the top.

"You are the promise for a more equal world," she told Barnard College graduates in her 2011 commencement speech. "You are our hope. . . . Make sure women's voices are heard and heeded, not overlooked and ignored. . . . Go home tonight and ask yourselves, 'What would I do if I weren't afraid?' And then go do it."[1]

During that famous speech, Sheryl cited a study that showed success and likeability are positively correlated with men and negatively correlated with women. This means that as men become more successful, people find them more likeable. But as women grow more successful, people like them less. It's a study she also cited in her viral 2010 TED Talk on how to increase the number of women in leadership positions.

That TED Talk put Sheryl on the map as a global force for female equality. In it, she shared a personal story about giving a talk at Facebook to more than one hundred people. Afterward, a young woman came up to her and said, "I learned something today. I learned I need to keep my hand up."[2]

Sheryl didn't quite understand. But then the young woman went on to explain that after the talk, Sheryl had said she would take two more questions. The young woman had her hand up, along with many other women. And Sheryl took two more questions. And then the young woman, along with the other women whose hands were raised, put her hand down. The men kept their hands up, and Sheryl took their questions.

"I thought to myself, 'Wow! If it's me who cares about this—obviously, giving the talk—and I can't even notice that the men's hands are still raised, how good are we at seeing that men are reaching for opportunities more than women?'" Sheryl said.[3]

One of Sheryl's consistent messages has been the importance of women believing in themselves, trusting themselves, and advocating for themselves. Too often, she believes, women unintentionally hold themselves back because of self-doubt, people pleasing, or hesitation to ask for what they truly want.

Her best-selling book *Lean In: Women, Work, and the Will to Lead* addresses these "internal obstacles" and how women can overcome them and put themselves forward for leadership opportunities.

The book has a companion nonprofit organization and website, offering resources like *Lean In* circles for women to connect with each other, practical tips and tools for self-advocacy, and discussion guides for people of all ages. The discussion guides offer self-exploration prompts in the form of questions like: "Have you ever felt as if you were ignored or silenced? Do you think that treatment was based on your gender? Why or why not?"[4]

Sheryl's second book also has a companion nonprofit organization and website with resources. This one, however, grew out of personal tragedy. In 2015, Sheryl became a widow at forty-five years old when her husband died suddenly. Facing life as a bereaved single mother of two young children, she began publicly expressing her grief and vulnerabilities, and privately writing in a journal about everything she was going through.

That journal eventually became the basis for *Option B: Facing Adversity, Building Resilience, and Finding Joy*, which she cowrote with psychologist Adam Grant.

Option B is a raw look at Sheryl's personal pain. It's also a handbook for navigating life's hardships, including illness, injury, divorce, and death. The book, along with its companion nonprofit and website, offers practical tools like how to ask for help, how to build a support network, and what to say to someone who's struggling. It also offers tips for processing grief, such as honoring your feelings as they are rather than trying to push them away, stay strong, or hold yourself to a timeline for healing.

"It might seem counterintuitive, but to move forward, you've got to do the exact thing you don't want to do. You've got to lean into the suck," explains the *Option B* website. "Leaning into the suck is like flowing with a thrashing wave instead of fighting against it. The wave is still powerful, but if you let yourself accept your feelings, that wave won't push you around quite so roughly."[5]

Dear Younger Me,

Believe in yourself and embrace your ambitions!

CHAPTER THIRTY
Dr. Maya Shankar
COGNITIVE BEHAVIORAL SCIENTIST

Dr. Maya Shankar. PHOTO BY KIRSTIN LARA GETCHELL, COURTESY OF DR. MAYA SHANKAR

Maya Shankar, PhD, is a cognitive neuroscientist who has created worldwide change by studying how and why people behave the way they do.

She started the White House's first-ever Social and Behavioral Sciences Team as a senior advisor to President Barack Obama, directing experts in helping federal agencies create new government policies based on research into human behavior.

The daughter of Indian immigrants, Maya went on to become the first behavioral science advisor to the United Nations and the global director of behavioral sciences at Google.

While Maya was getting her undergraduate degree at Yale University, *Glamour* magazine named her one of the country's Ten Most Impressive Women in College. She went on to earn a PhD from Oxford University, which she attended on a Rhodes Scholarship, and then a postdoctorate fellowship in cognitive neuroscience from Stanford University.

With those credentials, it might seem like Maya had a plan for her path to success and paved it intentionally. But, as she is fond of pointing out, nothing could be further from the truth.

"My journey was filled with a lot of challenges and confusion and anxiety and stress and many different twists and turns," she said in a keynote address at the 2019 UCLA Anderson Women's Summit.[1]

Maya's journey began when she was a six-year-old violin prodigy with a dream of attending the famed Juilliard School of Music. Indeed, she graduated from Juilliard's competitive precollege program, where renowned violinist Itzhak Perlman took her under his wing as a private student.

But then she injured a finger and tore a tendon in her hand, bringing her musical career to an untimely end. She was devastated. "That was the thing that got me into college," she remembered thinking. "Now I have super impostor syndrome; I don't even feel like I belong anymore at college, and I was pretty concerned that I had lost my little special spark."

But that spark ignited again later that summer, when Maya was helping her parents clean out their basement. She discovered a book by Steven Pinker called *The Language Instinct* and was fascinated to learn about the human brain's capacity to process and understand language.

"I just remember being blown away," she said, "because I was thinking this very simple trait that I've totally taken for granted is actually the result of really sophisticated cognitive machinery. Can you imagine what underlies things like mathematical processing, or falling in love?"

At that point, Maya said, she was hooked. "I thought, 'Okay, I think I've found potentially a new passion.'"

That new passion led her to study cognitive science at Yale. When she learned that select juniors and seniors had access to a laboratory where they conducted cognitive research using monkeys, she wanted in. She was only a freshman and wasn't allowed to apply. But that didn't stop her. She filled out a one-page application by writing five pages that pleaded her case, saying, essentially, "I'm willing to do the 6am shifts on Saturday morning in the dead of winter. . . . Please just give me, the freshman, a chance."

It worked. The professor gave her a chance, and she got to do research that paved the way for her PhD and postdoctorate fellowship.

"At every phase of my life," she said, "I'm thinking, 'Ah, now I can sit back, figured it out!'"

She had been studying cognitive science for fifteen years, and her path appeared clear. But then, standing in a dark laboratory scanning a human brain, she admitted to herself that she was feeling isolated and longed to be part of a team.

She reached out to the college professor who had taken a chance on her as a freshman. That professor told her about a behavioral scientist in the U.S. government who was studying how to get more parents to take advantage of free and reduced lunch programs for their children. He had figured out that the application forms were too long and cumbersome. So he came up with a way to transfer data from other programs the families were enrolled in, easing the application process and enabling more low-income children to access school meals.

"A lightbulb just went off in my head," Maya said, "and I thought, 'Oh man, that's the kind of work I want to be doing. I want to be taking the research that I've been learning about for the past many years and actually applying it to social problems to try to figure out if we can improve people's lives.'"

So she emailed the scientist and asked for his help. In that email, she did something she later came to regret. She wrote, "I know I'm not cool enough to work with the likes of [President] Obama, but if there's someone in state or local government, please let me know so I can connect with them."

Even though Maya had downplayed her value—something she now advises other women never to do—the researcher wrote back that he would be willing to introduce her to Obama's science advisor. It was just an informational interview, as there was no job available. But that didn't stop Maya from trying.

"I'm just going to go in there and basically tell him, 'Hey, I believe there should be a behavioral scientist in the White House, and I believe that person should be me,'" she said. "And that took a lot of confidence, right? Fake confidence, probably, at the time, but you know, if you act the part, sometimes it just works itself out."

And it did. She was hired to join the White House Office of Science and Technology Policy. She soon realized her work as a behavioral scientist could be far more effective in helping federal agencies if she had a dedicated team working with her.

"I can't tell you the number of times I was told I couldn't do this," she said. Everyone told her, "Look Maya, so many people who are way more powerful than you tried to do this. They weren't successful."

They also weren't Maya. She essentially knocked on the doors of dozens of federal agencies and experts, trying to convince them how valuable it would be to have a team of researchers dedicated to forming better federal policies using behavioral science.

In 2014, Obama established the Social and Behavioral Sciences Team and named Maya its leader.

"It was very much a start-up-in-your-parents'-basement type of feel," she said.

Thanks to Maya's leadership, the interagency group grew into a team of behavioral science experts that worked on dozens of projects to streamline federal programs, benefitting people across the country.

In 2016, with the election of President Donald Trump, Maya left the White House to become the first behavioral science advisor to the United Nations and then the first global director of behavioral sciences at Google. She went on to become the creator, executive producer, and host of the podcast *A Slight Change of Plans*, aptly named for her ability to blaze brand-new trails in the face of uncertainty and adversity. In 2021, Apple awarded her podcast Best Show of the Year.

"I just refused to look at the cookie-cutter profiles for my skill set," she said. "And I thought, 'Okay, what's the next big thing that I want to do?'"

Dear Younger Me,

Resist the urge to plan your future so much! There will be so many things that happen to you that derail your plans and are fully out of your control. Try and become comfortable with a constant state of uncertainty—it will serve you well as you navigate life's twists and turns.

CHAPTER THIRTY-ONE

Lateefah Simon

RACIAL JUSTICE ACTIVIST

Lateefah Simon. BART.GOV PHOTO

Lateefah Simon is a nationally recognized advocate for civil rights and racial justice. In 2003, she was the youngest-ever woman to receive a Genius Grant from the MacArthur Foundation, for advocating on behalf of at-risk girls struggling to stay off the streets and out of jail.

But in 1993, she was one of those girls.

At sixteen years old, Lateefah was a high school dropout with a full-time job at a fast-food chain and a juvenile record for shoplifting. While on probation, she was referred to the Center for Young Women's Development in California, an organization that uses peer counseling, job training, and other support services to help empower at-risk teens.

She quickly went from client to volunteer. She could identify with the girls who were struggling and was so successful at helping them that she was offered a position as outreach coordinator. She met teenage girls who were being trafficked and poured her energy into helping them build back their self-esteem and their lives.

When she was eighteen years old, Lateefah gave birth to a daughter and became a single mother. But she continued to help others who were struggling, and the following year she was named executive director at the center, heading up the organization that had helped empower her. She fought for employment training, childcare, and other services for teens.

She became so involved in the plight of marginalized young women, and so aware that the government was not helping them, that she started showing up at weekly municipal meetings, demanding to know what the city of Oakland, California, was going to do to support these young people. Her efforts caught the attention of then–city attorney Kamala Harris, who brought her on board to find ways to get these teens the support they needed.

In 2005, when Harris became the San Francisco district attorney, she chose Lateefah to lead a new program called Back on Track, an initiative to keep first-time drug offenders from winding up back in the juvenile justice system. Lateefah's work was so successful that Back on Track boasted a 10 percent recidivism rate, compared with 70 percent for people not enrolled in the program. It's now a national model for rehabilitation, used in cities across the country.

In 2009, *O, The Oprah Magazine* created its first-ever Power List of "remarkable visionaries who are flexing their muscles."[1] Lateefah made the list. That same year, she was appointed executive director of the Lawyers' Committee for Civil Rights of the San Francisco Bay area, which fights for the legal rights of marginalized people, including immigrants and refugees. She was one of the youngest-ever leaders of the group and was also one of the only nonlawyers.

Meanwhile, Lateefah continued visiting teen women in jail, helping them get the support services they needed. She also served as a role model. "I want people to know that a better life is possible," she told the *San Francisco Chronicle*. "I want them to know that no matter who you are or what you've done, you are due a process of transformation. You deserve another chance."[2]

The John F. Kennedy Presidential Library recognized Lateefah's work with a New Frontier Award in 2010. In presenting the award, Caroline Kennedy said, "Lateefah is bringing hope and inspiration to people of all ages who are struggling to overcome poverty and discrimination. We look to her inspiring example with hope and gratitude."[3]

Two years later, Lateefah met the man she calls the love of her life, who would become her husband and the father of her second daughter. Kevin Weston was a well-known journalist who helped people of color get jobs in the media. But on Father's Day 2014, Kevin passed away from leukemia. Even with health insurance, his hospital bills left Lateefah nearly $1 million in debt. She had to file for bankruptcy, and her personal situation highlighted the significant challenges of single mothers in the workforce. So she fought even harder for things like childcare subsidies and paid leave for caregivers.

Lateefah achieved all of this while being legally blind. Unable to drive because of her blindness, she relied on public transportation. But she felt it was too expensive for people who needed it the most. So she set out to change that. In 2016, she became the first Black board member of Bay Area Rapid Transit, where she worked to make public transportation more affordable for people who depended on it.

That same year, she was appointed by then-Governor Jerry Brown as a trustee for the California State University system, where she developed strategies for improving racial justice in higher education. One year later, at the age of forty, Lateefah graduated from Mills College in California. She had taken night and weekend classes while working full time. Her class chose her as the commencement speaker.

"We are cyclones. We are a collection of winds that are forceful and can never be stopped," she told her fellow Mills College graduates. "Be a blessing. be a physical manifestation of what a cyclone can be in human force."[4]

The following year, she gave another motivational speech, this time in a TEDx Talk encouraging advocacy in the Black community.

"We cannot move through or arrest our way or legislate our way out of the tarnish of nearly five hundred years of radicalized oppression with laws," she said. "It will take movement and it will take voice and I ask all of us to step back and stop waiting for that person to save us. 'Cause guess what? It's us. Let's go."[5]

Dear Younger Me,

Little Sister . . . choose you first. Be your own best friend. No one will love you more than you love yourself. Know that your body is yours to love—your face, ears, eyes—your smile and words are as perfect as your grandmother prayed them to be. You are smarter than you know, so put your head down and craft your vision and mold it into a life of joy. Be loud. Take up lots of space. Write like you speak, daily. Lastly, I want you to know to be gentle with yourself, understanding that you'll gain wisdom with each misstep. Dance, Lateefah, dance.

CHAPTER THIRTY-TWO

Erna Solberg

FORMER PRIME MINISTER

Erna Solberg. PHOTO BY TORBJØRN KJOSVOLD/FORSVARET

FROM 2013 TO 2021, ERNA SOLBERG SERVED AS THE PRIME minister of Norway, only the second woman ever to hold that position. Before she was elected prime minister, she served as minister of local government and regional development, where the media nicknamed her "Iron Erna," for her tough-minded, conservative approach, which included tightening immigration rules.

"When journalists give you a nickname, it's very difficult to get rid of it," she said after being elected prime minister in 2013, explaining that she had softened her approach a bit and become more focused on education, health, and jobs.[1]

"We thought that people would look upon us as care-taking and concerned with everyday life," she said. "But most people were seeing us as yes, good at running the economy, but not very interested in people's everyday life."[2]

People's everyday lives, especially the lives of women in low- and middle-income countries, was a major focus of Erna's administration. One of her personal passions has always been women's empowerment, including equality in education and the job market.

"When women are educated, they gain more influence and control of their lives," Erna said in a 2015 World Economic Forum speech entitled "How Can Investing in Women and Girls Accelerate Global Development beyond 2015?"[3]

"Better economic opportunities and stronger political participation," she said, "also strengthen their roles as agents of change and their ability to transform their societies for the better."[4]

Erna spoke about promoting women's equal access to job training and start-up businesses, including in the areas of agriculture and fisheries. She also spoke about securing land rights for women in developing countries. She highlighted the urgency and importance of women's empowerment and emphasized the devastating impacts of violence against women.

"The costs of gender discrimination and gender-based violence are high," she said. "Recent studies in a range of countries, including Norway, various EU countries, Vietnam and South Africa, show that the costs of violence against women and girls are huge, not only for the victims, but also for society as a whole."[5]

She closed her speech by saying, "I would also like to remind you that equality between women and men is a human right with its own merit. We must never trade that off."[6]

In 2014, Erna led Norway's financial backing of a new United Nations program to provide greater access to education for girls in Malawi, a country in southeast Africa. The program included health care, school meals, teacher training, antiviolence programs, and human rights education.

"If you invest in a girl," Erna wrote in a 2014 op-ed, "she feeds herself, educates future children, lifts up her community and propels her nation forward—charting a path that offers dignity for all in the process."[7]

Because of Erna's commitment to educating girls around the world, she was honored on International Women's Day in 2015 by Global Partnership for Education as one of fifteen Women Leading the Way for Girls' Education. Erna was among the select group of women who were "using their voices, leadership and influence to make progress for girls' education globally."[8]

Forbes magazine included Erna on its list of Power Women.

Starting in 2016, she cochaired the UN Secretary General's Advocacy Group for Sustainable Development Goals. One of those goals was fighting poverty, discrimination, and cultural biases that could keep girls all over the world from accessing educational opportunities.

Part of Erna's passion for educating girls comes from her own struggles with dyslexia in school. She was officially diagnosed at age sixteen, after getting low grades because teachers thought she wrote poorly and talked too much in school.

In 2017, after guiding Norway through an oil crisis and averting a recession, Erna was reelected to a second term as prime minister. She continued to fight for gender equality. When the COVID pandemic hit in 2020, she pointed out how it exposed deep fundamental flaws in worldwide approaches to poverty, health care, and education.

She also highlighted Norway's commitment to gender equality, and emphasized the need for other countries to follow suit in advocating for women's rights during the pandemic.

"We all know from experience that gender equality is smart economics," she said. "Equal access to high-quality education is vital for achieving gender parity in the labor market and equal participation in society."[9]

If countries don't encourage or promote employment opportunities for women, she said, that "means wasting half of a country's skills and capacity. Therefore, we will not be able to respond successfully to the pandemic or recover from it if women are left out of the equation."[10]

In addition to education and employment, Erna's other priorities have been humanitarian aid, sustainability, conflict resolution, cyber security, combating climate change, and cutting gas and oil emissions.

In 2018, she received the first Global Citizen World Leader Award for her international focus on creating positive change.

Dear Younger Me,

You can do it! You can handle more than you think. By taking responsibility and leadership at an early age, I learned to say yes to new opportunities, even though I didn't know how to deal with every aspect of the task in advance. I hope this gives you the courage to accept new challenges.

CHAPTER THIRTY-THREE
Dr. Sara Seager
ASTROPHYSICIST

Dr. Sara Seager. PHOTO BY ARAM BOGHOSIAN, COURTESY OF
DR. SARA SEAGER

SARA SEAGER, PHD, IS ON THE HUNT FOR LIFE OUTSIDE OF our solar system. She's so famous for her determination to find another Earth-like planet that NASA has dubbed her the "astronomical Indiana Jones."

Sara is a professor of planetary science, physics, aeronautics, and astronautics at the Massachusetts Institute of Technology and has received a Genius Grant from the MacArthur Foundation. She has been recognized for her research by magazines including *Popular Science, Discover, Nature*, and *Time*.

It all started when she was just a few years old. "I always loved the night sky," she said. One of her earliest memories is of looking up and wondering, "Why does the moon keep following me?" She remembers riding in the car and making note of the fact that "no matter how far we drove or which way we turned, the moon stayed fixated on me like a giant eye in the sky."[1]

Soon after, her father took her to a "star party," where amateur astronomers set up their telescopes and invited people to look through them. "When I first saw the moon through the telescope, I couldn't believe my eyes," she said. "A whole new world!"[2]

Then, when she was ten years old, she went on her first camping trip. She saw the dark night sky and what seemed like an endless number of stars. "What is out there?" she wondered. "Surely something giant and mysterious. I was astonished."[3]

When she was sixteen, she bought her first telescope. And then came a high school physics class where students had to calculate the exact distance and angle that would make a spring fly through the air and into a hole in a wooden board. Sara was fascinated when her equation sent the spring precisely where she calculated it would go. It was a lightbulb moment that showed her the power of combining an equation, a measurement, a calculation, and a prediction to achieve a desired result.

But even as Sara continued to deepen and develop her passion for astrophysics, she constantly struggled with feeling different. "In elementary school and high school, other kids thought I was weird," she said. "I wanted to join social outings but was rejected."[4]

Much later in life, Sara was diagnosed with autism. And while she finds social interactions difficult because "I am wired differently from the majority of people I interact with," she now sees being different from the crowd as one of her greatest assets.[5]

"Now, I'm comfortable being an outsider," she said. "This is important for breakthrough science—if I need approval from others about my innovative ideas, how could I create breakthroughs?"[6]

And Sara's breakthroughs have been many. She holds a PhD from Harvard University. She has led research teams working with data from space telescopes like Hubble. She led a rocket lab mission to Venus. Her specific area of expertise is the realm of exoplanets: planets that orbit stars other than the sun. She has already discovered thousands of them, and she is determined to discover a "Goldilocks" exoplanet—one that's not too hot and not too cold, with just the right conditions to sustain life.

"I believe that in our lifetime, we will be able to take children to a dark sky and point to a star and say, 'That star has a planet with signs of life in its atmosphere. That star has a planet like Earth,'" she said during a 2013 TEDx Talk. "And I am going to be devoting the rest of my life to making this happen."[7]

Sara also believes that eventually, those Earth-like exoplanets won't just be something we view with telescopes.

"I envision that our descendants, hundreds of years from now, will embark on an interstellar journey to other worlds," she said in another TED Talk two years later. "And they will look back at all of us as the generation who first found the Earth-like worlds."[8]

Sara leads international research teams involved with searching outer space for these signs of life and Earth-like worlds by examining biosignature gases—certain gases that accumulate in the atmosphere at levels that indicate life. She has written two textbooks on the topic of exoplanets and their atmospheres, and her research is responsible for laying the foundation for the entire field.

But initially, Sara was ridiculed by members of the scientific community, who thought her ideas were too far-fetched. But she trusted her instincts and her scientific mind.

"You have this immense curiosity," she said, "this stubbornness, this sort of resolute will that you will go forward no matter what other people say."[9]

She did go forward. And she proved the skeptics wrong.

In addition to researching biosignature gases, one of Sara's pioneering exoplanet projects is the Starshade, a giant screen that will be shot into space with a telescope. The flower-shaped screen will unfurl and temporarily block out the starlight that currently makes it impossible to actually see the light of exoplanets.

Right now, the search for exoplanets is "like looking for a firefly right next to a search light, when that firefly and searchlight are thousands of miles away," she said.[10]

The Starshade is intended to block out enough of the light to make the exoplanets visible.

For Sara, the search for life outside of our solar system is part of an innate drive to discover the endless possibilities that lay beyond what we can immediately see, feel, and know.

"Exploring is part of what it means to be human," she said. "The search for signs of life beyond Earth speaks to me as an explorer. Space is a place we can explore with telescopes and spacecraft, even if it is not easy or impossible for us humans to explore by physically going there."[11]

Dear Younger Me,

Being painfully different from others now will be one of your greatest future career strengths.

CHAPTER THIRTY-FOUR

Kathrine Switzer

ATHLETE AND ADVOCATE

Kathrine Switzer. PHOTO BY HAGEN HOPKINS

KATHRINE SWITZER MADE SPORTS HISTORY IN 1967 AS THE first woman to officially register for and run the Boston Marathon. At the time, it was a men's-only race, and as she was running, an angry official attacked her and tried to rip off her bib. He demanded she quit the race because she was a woman.

She kept running. The photo of that incident ignited a global uproar and became one of Time Life's 100 Photos That Changed the World.

But Kathrine never set out to make history. She was just a college girl who loved to run.

When Kathrine was in college, conventional wisdom was that women weren't built for long-distance running, that it wasn't medically advisable for them, and that it could damage their reproductive organs. Because of this, there was no women's cross country team at Syracuse University, so Kathrine trained unofficially with the men's team. When she told the coach she wanted to run the Boston Marathon, he told her women were too fragile to run marathons. But he told her if she could run the whole twenty-six-mile distance in practice, he would take her to Boston for the race.

She did it. The next day, he helped her register for the marathon. Since she registered using only her initials, K. V. Switzer, race officials had no idea that a woman had signed up to run.

"The thing I worried about most was courage," she wrote in her memoir, *Marathon Woman*. "Would I have the courage to keep running if it really hurt, if it got harder than I was used to, if Heartbreak Hill broke me? I was worried about maybe not having the courage if it got awful."[1]

It was snowing and sleeting on April 19, 1967, when she pinned number 261 onto her sweatshirt, and off she went. Around mile four, reporters on the back of the photo press truck began snapping pictures.

Suddenly, a man with an overcoat and felt hat appeared in the middle of the street, shaking his finger at her. "Moments later," she wrote, "I heard the scraping noise of leather shoes coming up fast behind me. . . . I jerked my head around quickly and looked square into the most vicious face I'd ever seen. A big man, a huge man, with bared teeth was set to pounce, and before I could react he grabbed my shoulder and flung me back, screaming, 'Get the hell out of my race and give me those numbers!' Then he swiped down my front, trying to rip off my bib number, just as I leaped backward from him."

Terrified, Kathrine kept running.

"If I quit," she wrote, "nobody would ever believe that women had the capability to run 26-plus miles. If I quit, everybody would say it was a publicity stunt. If I quit, it would set women's sports back, way back, instead of forward."

As she ran, it occurred to her that maybe running wasn't actually dangerous for women; maybe the notion that running would harm women's reproductive organs was just a myth; maybe the fact that there were no college sports for women at large universities was just because women had never been given the chance to prove they could excel at sports.

Maybe, she thought, if women were given these opportunities, they could feel their power and their capabilities.

"After what happened today," she wrote, "I felt responsible to create those opportunities. I felt elated, like I'd made a great discovery."

Four hours and twenty minutes later, the finish line came into view. Her feet were blistered and her socks were blood soaked. But she knew she had "stepped into a different life."

From that day on, she campaigned for women's equality in sports. In 1972, women were officially allowed to run the Boston Marathon. That same year, she led the charge to create the first-ever women's road race. She herself went on to run forty-two marathons, winning the New York City Marathon in 1974.

She then expanded the women's running boom to twenty-seven countries with the creation of the Avon International Running Circuit of women's races. More than one million women have participated, and the Avon Running Circuit, with Kathrine at the helm, helped to convince the International Olympic Committee to include a women's marathon for the first time in 1984.

Kathrine continues to inspire women around the world to be "fearless in the face of adversity," which is the slogan for her nonprofit organization called 261 Fearless. The organization takes its name from her bib number in that first Boston Marathon and, to Kathrine, is symbolic of women's empowerment. 261 Fearless organizes running clubs and events across the globe to help connect, support, and encourage women to know their own capabilities.

In 2011, Kathrine was inducted into the National Women's Hall of Fame for creating positive social change throughout her career.

In 2017, to celebrate the fiftieth anniversary of her historic run, Kathrine laced up once again for the Boston Marathon, wearing bib number 261. This time around, she used her full name. She was seventy years old, and she finished only twenty-four minutes over her time from half a century earlier. At the end of that race, officials from the Boston Athletic Association said they would retire her bib number, never again assigning it to any other runner, out of respect for Kathrine's barrier-breaking run, career, and life.

Dear Younger Me,

You don't have to have all the answers and do it all yourself. It's okay—in fact, it's a good thing—to ask someone you respect for help and advice. You're not showing weakness; you are adding to your strength.

CHAPTER THIRTY-FIVE

Tina Wells

ENTREPRENEUR

Tina Wells. PHOTO BY TAEA THALE, COURTESY OF TINA WELLS

Growing up, Tina Wells and her five younger siblings knew that Black History Month meant handmade coloring books from their father featuring Black heroes throughout history.

"We didn't grow up rich, but we grew up understanding our history," she wrote in a 2023 blog post.[1]

At the time, however, Tina and her siblings didn't appreciate the impact of what they were learning. "Back in the '90s, we made fun of his creation," she remembered. "We groaned every February 1, saying, 'Here Dad goes with that coloring book again!'"[2]

But those coloring books ended up having a powerful influence on Tina. She was especially encouraged by reading the story of Madam C. J. Walker, who rose up from poverty to create a line of hair-care products for Black women in the early 1900s. The daughter of former slaves, she became America's first Black female millionaire, known for creating business opportunities for Black women during a time of intense discrimination.

"When I read Madam Walker's story, I was encouraged by the idea that I could make money doing something I absolutely loved, even something others might even think was trite," Tina wrote. "Her story helped me lean into my creativity and set the stage for the work I'm doing now."[3]

That work includes being an entrepreneur, a best-selling author, a motivational speaker, and a brand-builder who helps people connect with what matters most to them.

She started her first company when she was only sixteen years old, offering product feedback and reviews for businesses from a teenager's perspective. She joined forces with one of her college professors, built a business plan, and created the Buzz Marketing Group, an award-winning marketing agency that evolved to serve clients such as Apple, Dell, American Eagle, the Oprah Winfrey Network, and Johnson & Johnson.

Tina spent the next two decades growing a seven-figure business, living what she thought was her dream. But the constant hustle was taking its toll. There was no time for rest or recovery. She started to feel depleted, and it only got worse.

"I was experiencing so much anxiety, panic, hair loss, stomach pains—you name it," Tina said. "It was clear something was going on, and I really needed to pause and get it sorted out."[4]

The stress got so bad that Tina began to dread going to the office. The company she had worked so long and so hard to build was becoming her biggest source of mental and physical fatigue and burnout. She decided to close up shop.

"But that was the best thing to ever happen to me!" Tina said.[5] In that period of down time, she took stock of what brought her joy. She let go of what didn't. She gave herself time to rethink her work and her life. She reconnected with her authentic self and discovered her love of writing.

Within just a few months, she wrote seven middle-grade fiction books featuring strong female characters of color and sold them to a publisher. It was important to Tina "for young readers to see themselves reflected in those characters, because you never know how that influences a child to think about what they can or can't do."[6]

In this new phase of her life, Tina felt "totally in the flow" and "had never been happier personally or professionally."[7]

When she dissected the method she had used for creating this happiness, she realized it could be broken down into four phases: Preparation, inspiration, recreation, and transformation. These steps became the framework for her signature work-life harmony formula that she now calls the Elevation Approach.

"I created this method to help me achieve work-life harmony since the idea of balance felt antiquated. We're never equal halves work and personal, so I needed to create a method that would allow me to live my best life," she said.[8]

The Elevation Approach included concrete actions like creating rituals, decluttering, releasing what was weighing her down, and developing a personal spiritual practice. It worked so well for her that she wrote a whole book about it, which is now helping people all over the world find greater fulfillment in their lives.

"Work-life harmony allows us to achieve our goals while making sure we're well enough to enjoy them," she explains. "What's the point of getting what we want if we're too tired, irritated, and anxious to enjoy it?"[9]

Tina now heads up RLVNT Media, the multimedia marketing company she founded. She has been honored with *Cosmopolitan* magazine's Fun Fearless Phenom Award and recognized as one of *Inc.* magazine's 30 under 30, *Billboard* magazine's 30 under 30, and *Essence* magazine's 40 under 40. *Fast Company* listed her among the 100 Most Creative People in Business.

Her board positions include the United Nations Foundation's Global Entrepreneurs Council, and she has served as the academic director for Wharton Business School's Leadership in the Business World Program.

In addition to creating the Elevation Approach, Tina also created the companion *Elevation Tribe*, a leadership publication dedicated to helping women of color launch and grow their businesses. She wants her entrepreneurial journey to serve as inspiration to other women looking to gain traction and make a difference in the world.

"I'm really aware of what it means to show up, what it means to create representation, what it means to create opportunities for other people," she said.[10]

Dear Younger Me,

It's okay if no one really understands what you "do" for a living. It's okay if people question your path, your vision, and your passion. It will all make sense one day, and you'll be so happy you followed your own path. Trust yourself always.

AFTERWORD

I AM DEEPLY GRATEFUL TO THE THIRTY-FIVE TRAILBLAZING women who carved out time from their busy lives to contribute these exclusive nuggets of wisdom to their younger selves and, by extension, to you.

I learned so much from them. But I also learned from many of the women who didn't participate in the book—or at least, who didn't participate in the way that I had initially requested.

I certainly wasn't surprised when I didn't hear back from some of the women, given that the ones I reached out to are world famous and extremely busy. My protocol was to do a gentle follow-up nudge a month or so later, and then, if I didn't hear back, I'd assume it was a pass.

But in other cases, the passes themselves delivered the lessons. I've always had a hard time saying no, often to the point of burnout and depletion.

Here's an email I received after reaching out to Malala Yousafzai, the Pakistani activist and 2014 Nobel Peace Prize laureate who was shot by the Taliban for opposing restrictions on female education.

Hi Elisa,

Hope all is well and nice to hear from you. We really appreciate you reaching out to us with this opportunity, but at this time Malala is unavailable to participate. Thanks so much for thinking of Malala and wanting to provide a safe space to discuss girls' education with your audiences. We would be happy to keep in touch if there are any future opportunities to work together. Best of luck with the book.

It was, as we say in publishing, a "champagne rejection": a master class in politely drawing boundaries and a perfect blueprint for an overgiver who was, at the time, struggling with overextending herself.

Here's what I wrote back:

I completely understand and I thank you for getting back to me. I have received several truly heartfelt responses from women politely declining. Including this one! I'm so impressed by the kind and personal declines that I'm receiving from those who are unable to participate. So much so, in fact, that I'm mulling over the idea of including a few of them in an afterword. I'm thinking it might be a great way to show young readers how to draw boundaries, not take too much on their plates, and warmly pass on things that would feel like too much. Okay to use your response in this way?

Not only did the folks at the Malala Fund say yes, they also wrote:

We are extremely grateful for your support and also your work to elevate important issues for girls and young women everywhere.

When I reached out to fellow introvert Susan Cain, the bestselling author of *Bittersweet* and *Quiet*, I heard back from her assistant, Renee:

> *Thanks so much for the kind invitation. As much as Susan would love to contribute, she just doesn't have a moment free. Thank you for thinking of her. Good luck to you with your book!*

When I told her about my plan to include this champagne rejection in my book, she wrote back: *Wow. I am honored!*
So was I.

From the office of Gloria Steinem:

> *This looks great but unfortunately Gloria needs to decline. She's working almost exclusively on her book right now and isn't adding anything to her plate. Even the small things truly add up. Thanks for understanding and best wishes!*

These responses were becoming guideposts along my path to learning what I have come to call the Divine No.

This book was a labor of love, but it took way more time and energy than any other project thus far. I could feel myself burning out. Something had to change. It was a perfect teaching tool to practice what I now realize is a critical form of self-care: to drop inside and get completely clear on my priorities, rather than saying yes to opportunities that were not completely aligned with my goals or capacities.

Every time we give ourselves permission to activate our Divine No, we honor and make space for a Divine Yes.

As I write this afterword, on the eve of my deadline, I am grateful for this additional wisdom that came disguised as rejection. Blessings often do.

Thank you for walking with me through these pages. I'm sending you support and solidarity for all of your Divine Yesses to come.

LEARN MORE
Online Resources for Further Exploration

Manal al-Sharif
https://manalsharif.wordpress.com/

Dr. Katrin Amunts
https://www.fz-juelich.de/profile/amunts_k

Human Brain Project: https://www.humanbrainproject.eu/en/

Renae Bluitt
https://www.renaebluitt.com/

May Boeve
350.org: https://350.org/

Dr. Joan Borysenko
https://joanborysenko.com/

Gail Koziara Boudreaux
Elevance Health: https://www.elevancehealth.com/who-we
-are/senior-leadership/gail-boudreaux

The Business Council: https://businesscouncil.com/

Dr. Tara Brach
https://www.tarabrach.com/

Dr. Krystyna Chiger
Yad Vashem, The World Holocaust Remembrance Center:
https://www.yadvashem.org/education/educational-mate
rials/books/girl-green.html

María Soledad Cisternas Reyes
United Nations appointment: https://www.un.org/sg/en/con
tent/sg/personnel-appointments/2017-06-20/ms-mar
%C3%ADa-soledad-cisternas-reyes-chile-special-envoy

ABA International Human Rights Award: https://www
.americanbar.org/groups/international_law/international
-projects/international-human-rights-award/

Dr. Dianne Chong
Engineer Girl: https://www.engineergirl.org/116487/Dianne
-Chong

National Academy of Engineering: https://www.nae.edu/

Dr. Johnnetta Betsch Cole
Spelman College: https://www.spelman.edu/about-us/office
-of-the-president/past-presidents/johnnetta-cole

Bennett College: https://www.bennett.edu/news/dr-johnnetta
-betsch-cole-speak-bennett-colleges-founders-day-convo
cation-sunday-september-10-2017/

Scholarship America: https://scholarshipamerica.org/

National Museum of African Art: https://africa.si.edu/

American Alliance of Museums: https://www.aam-us.org/

National Council of Negro Women: https://ncnw.org/

ATHENA International: https://www.athenainternational.org/

Ertharin Cousin
Food Systems for the Future: https://www.fsfinstitute.net /ertharin

Feeding America: https://www.feedingamerica.org/

United Nations Food and Agriculture: https://www.fao.org /home/en

United Nations World Food Programme: https://www.wfp.org/

Melinda Emerson
https://succeedasyourownboss.com/

Mackenzie Feldman
Re:wild Your Campus: https://www.rewildyourcampus.org/

U.S. Right to Know: Monsanto Papers: https://usrtk.org /monsanto-papers/

Dr. Christine Figgener
https://www.seaturtlebiologist.com/

Sea Turtle video: https://www.youtube.com/watch?v=4wH 878t78bw&t=304s

Beth Ford
Land O'Lakes: https://www.landolakesinc.com/

Gabby Giffords
GIFFORDS: https://giffords.org/

Julia Gillard
https://www.juliagillard.com.au/

Beyond Blue: https://www.beyondblue.org.au/

Global Institute for Women's Leadership: https://www.kcl
.ac.uk/giwl/who/who-we-are

Dr. Temple Grandin
https://www.templegrandin.com/

National Women's Hall of Fame: https://www.womenofthe
hall.org/

Maura Healey
https://maurahealey.com/

Human Rights Campaign: https://www.hrc.org/

S. E. Hinton
https://www.sehinton.com/

Janice Bryant Howroyd
https://askjbh.com/

ActOne Group: https://www.actonegroup.com/about.aspx

Dr. Laurie Marker
Cheetah Conservation Fund: https://cheetah.org/

Midori
https://www.midori-violin.com/

Julia Parsons
Veterans Breakfast Club: https://veteransbreakfastclub.org
/julia-parsons/

Nancy Pelosi
https://pelosi.house.gov/

Kaitlin Roig-DeBellis
https://kaitlinroigdebellis.org/

Classes4Classes: https://classes4classes.org/

Buffy Sainte-Marie
http://buffysainte-marie.com/

Sheryl Sandberg
Lean In: https://leanin.org/

Option B: https://optionb.org/

Dr. Maya Shankar
https://mayashankar.com/

Lateefah Simon
https://www.lateefahsimon.com/

Erna Solberg
https://erna.no/

Global Partnership for Education:
https://www.globalpartnership.org/

Dr. Sara Seager
https://www.saraseager.com/

Kathrine Switzer
https://kathrineswitzer.com/

261 Fearless: https://www.261fearless.org/

Tina Wells
https://tinawells.com/

NOTES

CHAPTER ONE: MANAL AL-SHARIF

1. "The False Promise of Saudi Reform: A Conversation with Manal Al-Sharif," Oslo Freedom Forum, September 28, 2018, https://www.youtube.com/watch?v=QLBRZQ4quEM.

2. "The False Promise of Saudi Reform."

3. Manal al-Sharif, "Once Women Take the Wheel, Saudi Arabia Will Never Be the Same," *Washington Post*, October 5, 2017, https://www.washingtonpost.com/news/global-opinions/wp/2017/10/05/once-women-take-the-wheel-saudi-arabia-will-never-be-the-same/.

4. Al-Sharif, "Once Women Take the Wheel."

5. "The False Promise of Saudi Reform."

6. "The False Promise of Saudi Reform."

7. "Manal Al-Sharif: 'It Wasn't about Driving a Car. It Was about Driving Our Own Destiny,'" Women of the World, April 10, 2019, https://www.youtube.com/watch?v=gAGDGQhUKes.

CHAPTER TWO: DR. KATRIN AMUNTS

1. Katrin Amunts, email message to the author, February 15, 2023.

2. Amunts, email message to the author.

3. Amunts, email message to the author.

4. "Katrin Amunts Shares Her Fascination for the Human Brain," European Commission, March 29, 2017, https://digital-strategy.ec.europa.eu/en/news/katrin-amunts-shares-her-fascination-human-brain.

5. "Showcasing STEM Women in Medical Science," News-Medical Life Sciences, February 11, 2022, https://www.news-medical.net/news/20220211/Showcasing-STEM-Women-in-Medical-Science.aspx.

6. "Showcasing STEM Women in Medical Science."

7. "Showcasing STEM Women in Medical Science."

8. "Katrin Amunts Shares Her Fascination for the Human Brain."

Chapter Three: Renae Bluitt

1. Dominique Fluker, "A Documentary Exploring the Passionate Pursuits of Black Women Entrepreneurs Premiers on Netflix Today—Here's Why You Should Tune In," *Forbes*, February 4, 2020, https://www.forbes.com/sites/dominiquefluker/2020/02/04/she-did-that/?sh=779e0dba6c8f.

2. Renae Bluitt website, https://www.renaebluitt.com/.

3. "Netflix Premieres First Ever Documentary about Black Women CEOs," *Black Business*, February 12, 2020, https://www.blackbusiness.com/2020/02/netflix-premieres-she-did-that-documentary-black-women-ceo-renae-bluitt.html.

4. "Netflix Premieres First Ever Documentary about Black Women CEOs."

5. Claudia Johnson, "From Blog to Film: This Woman Is Telling the Story of Successful Black Women Entrepreneurs," *Black Enterprise*, February 18, 2018, https://www.blackenterprise.com/from-blog-to-film-how-this-woman-is-bringing-the-story-of-women-entrepreneurs/.

6. Johnson, "From Blog to Film."

Chapter Four: May Boeve

1. May Boeve, email message to the author, February 9, 2023.

2. Boeve, email message to the author.

3. 350.org website, https://350.org/.

4. "Keystone XL resistance," 350.org, 2011, https://350.org/10-years/.

5. Boeve, email message to the author.

6. Charlotte Alter, "Forming Alliances in the Fight against Climate Change," *Time*, May 28, 2015, https://time.com/3896409/ngl-may-boeve/.

7. "Florida Congressman and Director of Leading Campaign Against Climate Change to Receive 2017 John F. Kennedy New Frontier Awards," John F. Kennedy Library, press release, 2017, https://www.jfklibrary.org/about-us/news-and-press/press-releases/2017-new-frontier-award-winners.

8. "New Frontier Award Honoree May Boeve on Fossil Fuel 'Disruption,'" John F. Kennedy Library, November 17, 2017, https://www.youtube.com/watch?v=mrBQrvZNTww.

9. "New Frontier Award Honoree May Boeve on Fossil Fuel 'Disruption.'"

10. "New Frontier Award Honoree May Boeve on Fossil Fuel 'Disruption.'"

CHAPTER FIVE: DR. JOAN BORYSENKO

1. All quotes in this chapter from Joan Borysenko, email message to the author, May 7, 2003.

CHAPTER SIX: GAIL KOZIARA BOUDREAUX

1. "Gail Koziara Boudreaux '82," Dartmouth College Athletics, October 12, 2015, https://dartmouthsports.com/news/2015/10/12/210418001.aspx.

2. Curtis Eichelberger, "Gail Koziara Boudreaux: From the Basketball Court to the Boardroom," National Collegiate Athletics Association, 2016, https://www.ncaa.org/sports/2016/2/2/gail-koziara-boudreaux-from-the-basketball-court-to-the-boardroom.aspx.

3. Eichelberger, "Gail Koziara Boudreaux."

4. Eichelberger, "Gail Koziara Boudreaux."

5. "Billie Jean King Introduces 2018 Billie Jean King Leadership Award," Women's Sports Foundation, August 25, 2020, https://www.youtube.com/watch?v=FBHuyKQ2G8s.

6. Corbin McGuire, "2022 Theodore Roosevelt Award: Gail Koziara Boudreaux," National Collegiate Athletics Association, January 13, 2022, https://www.ncaa.org/news/2022/1/13/media-center-2022-theodore-roosevelt-award-gail-koziara-boudreaux.aspx.

7. "Business Council Elects Gail K. Boudreaux as Chair," Business Wire, February 8, 2023, https://finance.yahoo.com/news/business-council-elects-gail-k-110000517.html.

CHAPTER SEVEN: DR. TARA BRACH

1. Tara Brach, email message to the author, February 20, 2023.

2. Brach, email message to the author.

3. Brach, email message to the author.

4. Brach, email message to the author.

5. Tara Brach, "RAIN: A Practice of Radical Compassion," https://www.tarabrach.com/rain/.

6. Same Mowe, "Wake Up from Unworthiness: An Interview with Tara Brach," *Spirituality & Health*, 2015, https://www.spiritualityhealth.com/articles/2015/09/01/wake-unworthiness/.

7. "Do You Have Spiritual Friends? The Joy and Nourishment that Comes from Fellowship on the Path," *Sounds True*, April 24, 2023, https://join.soundstrue.com/watch-the-special-event-with-jack-and-tara-sounds-true/.

8. Tara Brach, email message to subscribers, April 25, 2023.

9. Tara Brach, "Embodied Presence—Coming Home to Ourselves," https://www.tarabrach.com/part-1-refuge-wilderness-embodied-presence/.

CHAPTER EIGHT: DR. KRYSTYNA CHIGER

1. Unless otherwise noted, all quotes from Krystyna Chiger are from a telephone conversation with author, December 12, 2018.

2. Krystyna Chiger, email message to the author, June 8, 2023.

3. Chiger, email message to the author.

CHAPTER NINE: MARÍA SOLEDAD CISTERNAS REYES

1. María Soledad Cisternas Reyes, "My Journey in Advancing the Rights of Persons with Disabilities in Chile," *Practice*, May/June 2022, https://clp.law.harvard.edu/knowledge-hub/magazine/issues/global-disability-cause-lawyering/my-journey-in-advancing-the-rights-of-persons-with-disabilities-in-chile/.

2. Cisternas Reyes, "My Journey in Advancing the Rights of Persons with Disabilities in Chile."

3. Cisternas Reyes, "My Journey in Advancing the Rights of Persons with Disabilities in Chile."

4. Cisternas Reyes, "My Journey in Advancing the Rights of Persons with Disabilities in Chile."

5. "ABA Presents International Human Rights Award to Professor," *Legal News*, November 16, 2022, https://legalnews.com/oakland/1517568%20Legalnews.com.

6. "ABA Presents International Human Rights Award to Professor."

CHAPTER TEN: DR. DIANNE CHONG

1. "Interview with Dianne Chong," Leadership for Engineers, http://leadershipforengineers.com/index.php/interview-with-dianne-chong/.

2. "Interview with Dianne Chong."

3. "Interview with Dianne Chong."

4. "Dianne Chong (Retired) of Boeing, on Materials Innovation in Industry," Materials Research Society, August 16, 2017, https://www.youtube.com/watch?v=6qWVEZ7O9Lg.

5. "Interview with Dianne Chong."

6. Stacy Nguyen, "Our Top 10 Burning Questions with Dianne Chong," *Northwest Asian Weekly*, November 23, 2011, https://nwasian weekly.com/2011/11/our-top-10-burning-questions-with-dianne -chong/.

7. "Interview with Dianne Chong."

8. Dianne Chong, email message to the author, February 23, 2023.

9. "Interview with Dianne Chong."

10. Nguyen, "Our Top 10 Burning Questions with Dianne Chong."

CHAPTER ELEVEN: DR. JOHNNETTA BETSCH COLE

1. Johnnetta Cole, email message to the author, May 2, 2023.

2. "Dear Young Students: An Open Letter from Dr. Johnnetta Cole," Scholarship America, June 9, 2021, https://www.youtube.com /watch?v=dY8IeHocJ78.

3. "Dear Young Students: An Open Letter from Dr. Johnnetta Cole."

4. "Dear Young Students: An Open Letter from Dr. Johnnetta Cole."

5. "Dr. Johnnetta Betsch Cole: 2015 AAM General Session Keynote Address," American Alliance of Museums, April 27, 2015, https://www .youtube.com/watch?v=TmROOwIIVYM.

6. "Dr. Johnnetta Betsch Cole: 2015 AAM General Session Keynote Address."

7. "Dr. Johnnetta Betsch Cole: 2015 AAM General Session Keynote Address."

8. "Renowned Educator, Author Dr. Johnnetta Cole Joins Ranks of Global Award Recipients," ATHENA International, August 18, 2022, https://www.athenainternational.org/news/614530/Renowned-Educa tor-Author-Dr.-Johnnetta-Cole-Joins-Ranks-of-Global-Award-Recip ients.htm.

9. "Renowned Educator, Author Dr. Johnnetta Cole Joins Ranks of Global Award Recipients."

CHAPTER TWELVE: ERTHARIN COUSIN

1. Ertharin Cousin, "Ending Global Hunger: Yes We Can," TEDx, November 17, 2022, https://www.youtube.com/watch?v=QRRRIwt8b8A.

2. Cousin, "Ending Global Hunger: Yes We Can."

3. "Power with Purpose: Ertharin Cousin," Devex, April 10, 2017, https://www.youtube.com/watch?v=ZKpLPT8OT1I.

4. "Power with Purpose: Ertharin Cousin."

5. Cousin, "Ending Global Hunger: Yes We Can."

6. Cousin, "Ending Global Hunger: Yes We Can."

Chapter Thirteen: Melinda Emerson

1. Steve Strauss, "Exclusive Interview with NY Times Blogger, Host of #SmallBizChat, @SmallBizLady—Melinda Emerson," *ZenBusiness*, December 13, 2021, https://www.zenbusiness.com/blog/exclusive-interview-with-ny-times-blogger-host-of-smallbizchat-smallbizlady-melinda-emerson/.

2. "Melinda Emerson 'SmallBizLady': A Beacon of Hope for Small Businesses across America," CIO Views, April 2022, https://cioviews.com/melinda-emerson-smallbizlady-a-beacon-of-hope-for-small-businesses-across-america-4/.

3. "Melinda Emerson 'SmallBizLady: A Beacon of Hope'"

4. "Melinda Emerson 'SmallBizLady' on Her Mission to End Small Business Failure!" *World's Leaders*, https://worldsleaders.com/melinda-emerson-melinda-emersonsmallbizlady-on-her-mission-to-end-small-business-failure/.

5. Strauss, "Exclusive Interview."

6. "Melinda Emerson 'SmallBizLady' on Her Mission."

7. "Melinda Emerson 'SmallBizLady' on Her Mission."

8. "Melinda Emerson 'SmallBizLady': A Beacon of Hope."

Chapter Fourteen: Mackenzie Feldman

1. All quotes in this chapter from Mackenzie Feldman, email message to the author, April 3, 2023.

Chapter Fifteen: Dr. Christine Figgener

1. Christine Figgener, telephone call with the author, August 2019.

2. "The Sea Turtle with a Straw in Its Nostril—'No' to Single-Use Plastic," Sea Turtle Biologist, August 10, 2015, https://www.youtube.com/watch?v=4wH878t78bw.

3. Footprint, "Footprint Launches Non-Profit Foundation to Promote Positive Global Change through Sustainability Education and Engagement," PR Newswire, April 20, 2020, https://www.prnewswire.com/news-releases/footprint-launches-non-profit-founda

tion-to-promote-positive-global-change-through-sustainability-educa
tion-and-engagement-301043539.html.

4. Chloe Mei Espinosa, email message to the author, April 23, 2023.

5. Christine Figgener, email message to the author, August 2019.

6. Figgener, telephone call with the author.

CHAPTER SIXTEEN: BETH FORD

1. David Gelles, "Before She Was CEO, She Cleaned Toilets. 'How Wonderful Is That?'" *New York Times*, May 29, 2021, https://www.nytimes.com/2021/05/29/business/beth-ford-land-o-lakes-corner-office.html.

2. Gelles, "Before She Was CEO, She Cleaned Toilets."

3. "On Purpose: A Conversation with Land O'Lakes CEO Beth Ford," Zoetis, August 16, 2021, https://www.youtube.com/watch?v=ipBPP60gZoo.

4. Julia Carpenter, "A New First for LGBTQ Business Leaders," CNN Business, July 27, 2018, https://money.cnn.com/2018/07/27/news/companies/lgbtq-ceos/index.html.

5. Carpenter, "A New First for LGBTQ Business Leaders."

6. Stephanie Vozza, "Beth Ford Wants to Change the Narrative about Rural America," *Fast Company*, June 8, 2022, https://www.fastcompany.com/90753688/beth-ford-change-narrative-rural-america.

7. "Land O'Lakes CEO Beth Ford Says 'Bring Your Best Self to Work,'" *Fortune*, February 19, 2019, https://fortune.com/videos/watch/Land-OLakes-CEO-Beth-Ford-Says-Bring-Your-Best-Self-To-Work/11176ee7-ddd3-453a-8555-3e48770a05c1.

8. "Land O'Lakes CEO Says 'Bring Your Best Self to Work.'"

9. "Land O'Lakes CEO Says 'Bring Your Best Self to Work.'"

CHAPTER SEVENTEEN: GABBY GIFFORDS

1. Gabby Giffords, "10 Years Ago, a Gunman Tried to Silence Me," *New York Times*, January 8, 2021, https://www.nytimes.com/2021/01/08/opinion/gabby-giffords-shooting-capitol-attack.html.

2. James Crugnale, "Debbie Wasserman Schultz Reads Gabrielle Giffords' Resignation Letter," Mediaite, January 25, 2012, https://www.mediaite.com/tv/debbie-wasserman-schultz-reads-gabrielle-giffords-resignation-letter/.

3. "Gabby Giffords on Moving Forwards," *CBS Sunday Morning*, July 17, 2022, https://www.cbsnews.com/video/gabby-giffords-on-moving-forwards/.

4. "Watch: Gabby Giffords' Full Speech at the 2020 Democratic National Convention," *PBS NewsHour*, August 20, 2020, https://www.youtube.com/watch?v=1_QvvZOi_74.

5. "Watch: President Biden Awards Medal of Freedom to Simone Biles, Gabby Giffords and Others," *PBS NewsHour*, July 7, 2022, https://www.pbs.org/newshour/politics/watch-live-president-biden-awards-medal-of-freedom-to-simone-biles-denzel-washington-and-others.

6. "Watch: President Biden Awards Medal of Freedom."

7. "Gabby Giffords on Moving Forwards."

CHAPTER EIGHTEEN: JULIA GILLARD

1. Michelle Penelope King, "Julia Gillard, Australia's First Female Prime Minister on Leadership, Education and the Misogyny Speech," *Forbes*, September 17, 2019, https://www.forbes.com/sites/michelleking/2019/09/17/julia-gillard-australias-first-female-prime-minister-on-leadership-education-and-the-misogyny-speech/?sh=6b141a026d1e.

2. King, "Julia Gillard, Australia's First Female Prime Minister."

3. "Julia Gillard on Her New Book: Women & Leadership: Real Lives, Real Lessons," Women and Leadership New Zealand, September 10, 2020, https://womenandleadership.co.nz/julia-gillard-interview-women-leadership.html.

4. Allison Beard, "Life's Work: An Interview with Julia Gillard," *Harvard Business Review*, December 2019, https://hbr.org/2019/11/lifes-work-an-interview-with-julia-gillard.

5. Beard, "Life's Work."

6. Beard, "Life's Work."

7. Beard, "Life's Work."

8. King, "Julia Gillard, Australia's First Female Prime Minister."

CHAPTER NINETEEN: DR. TEMPLE GRANDIN

1. "Temple Grandin Inducted into Colorado Women's Hall of Fame," Where Food Comes From, March 8, 2012, https://web.archive.org/web/20131228000859/http://www.wherefoodcomesfrom.com/article/2281/Temple-Grandin-Inducted-into-Colorado-Womens-Hall-of-Fame#.Ur4WnR3go1I.

2. Temple Grandin, "How Does Visual Thinking Work in the Mind of a Person with Autism? A Personal Account," Grandin.com, 2009, https://www.grandin.com/inc/visual.thinking.mind.autistic.person.html.

3. Temple Grandin, "The World Needs All Kinds of Minds," TED, February 2010, https://www.ted.com/talks/temple_grandin_the_world_needs_all_kinds_of_minds.

4. Temple Grandin, "About Temple Grandin," https://www.temple grandin.com/.

5. Temple Grandin, "Everything in My Mind Works Like a Search Engine Set for the Image Function," Blank on Blank, https://blankon blank.org/interviews/temple-grandin-visualizing-autism-aspergers-cat tle-nerds/.

6. Grandin, "Everything in My Mind Works Like a Search Engine."

7. Grandin, "Everything in My Mind Works Like a Search Engine."

8. Jennifer Dimas, "Temple Grandin named to the National Women's Hall of Fame," SOURCE, February 10, 2017, https://source.colostate.edu/temple-grandin-named-national-womens-hall-fame/.

CHAPTER TWENTY: MAURA HEALEY

1. Steve LeBlanc, "Massachusetts' Healey Is 1st Lesbian Elected Governor in US," AP News, November 8, 2022, https://apnews.com/article/2022-midterm-elections-abortion-charlie-baker-don ald-trump-eed9407d66e03dd87051e46321a36f6f.

2. John Casey, "Massachusetts's Maura Healey on Becoming the First Lesbian Governor." *Advocate*, December 21, 2022, https://www.advocate.com/politics/2022/12/21/massachusettss-maura-healey-be coming-first-lesbian-governor.

3. Casey, "Massachusetts's Maura Healey on Becoming the First Lesbian Governor."

4. Casey, "Massachusetts's Maura Healey on Becoming the First Lesbian Governor."

5. Michelle Garcia, "Healey Elected First Out State Attorney General," *Advocate*, November 4, 2014, https://www.advocate.com/politics/election/2014/11/04/results-healey-elected-first-out-state-attorney-general.

6. Ellen O'Regan, "Granddaughter of Cork Emigrant Becomes First Openly Lesbian Governor in U.S.," Echo LIVE, November 9, 2022, https://www.echolive.ie/corknews/arid-41002724.html.

7. Casey, "Massachusetts's Maura Healey on Becoming the First Lesbian Governor."

8. Casey, "Massachusetts's Maura Healey on Becoming the First Lesbian Governor."

9. Casey, "Massachusetts's Maura Healey on Becoming the First Lesbian Governor."

10. Casey, "Massachusetts's Maura Healey on Becoming the First Lesbian Governor."

CHAPTER TWENTY-ONE: S. E. HINTON

1. Nina Laski, "S. E. Hinton Celebrates 'The Outsiders' 50th Anniversary," YouTube, April 30, 2017, https://www.youtube.com/watch?v=JvQ4GIYilizg.

2. Tom Simon 14, "S. E. Hinton on Location in Her Hometown of Tulsa, Oklahoma," YouTube, August 23, 2020, https://www.youtube.com/watch?v=JYaVcFi1R_Y.

3. "Oklahoma Writers: S. E. Hinton," Oklahoma Historical Society, 2011, https://www.okhistory.org/historycenter/writers/bio.php?lname=Hinton&fname=S.%20E.

4. Rocco Staino, "Interview with S. E. Hinton," YouTube, July 1, 2019, https://www.youtube.com/watch?v=Cr_Npz9ZOKo.

5. "Oklahoma Writers: S. E. Hinton."

6. Tom Simon 14, "S. E. Hinton on Location."

7. Staino, "Interview with S. E. Hinton."

8. Tom Simon 14, "S. E. Hinton on Location."

CHAPTER TWENTY-TWO: JANICE BRYANT HOWROYD

1. Denise Hamilton, "Personnel Exec Places Her Faith in Customer Service," *Los Angeles Times*, June 22, 1997, https://www.latimes.com/archives/la-xpm-1997-06-22-fi-5980-story.html.

2. Janice Bryant Howroyd, "Empowerment Advice from the First Black Woman to Start a Billion-Dollar Company," *Fast Company*, September 25, 2019, https://www.fastcompany.com/90408529/business-leader-janice-bryant-howroyd-on-empowering-others.

3. Howroyd, "Empowerment Advice."

4. Howroyd, "Empowerment Advice."

5. Howroyd, "Empowerment Advice."

6. Howroyd, "Empowerment Advice."

7. Howroyd, "Empowerment Advice."
8. Howroyd, "Empowerment Advice."

Chapter Twenty-Three: Dr. Laurie Marker

1. Peter Fimrite, "How a Napa Winemaker Became One of the World's Top Cheetah Experts," *San Francisco Chronicle*, October 28, 2014, https://www.sfgate.com/science/article/How-a-California-wine maker-became-one-of-the-5853377.php.
2. Laurie Marker, "Who We Are," Cheetah Conservation Fund, https://cheetah.org/about/who-we-are/dr-laurie-marker/.
3. Laurie Marker, "What If We Lost the Cheetah?" TEDx, June 2, 2013, https://www.youtube.com/watch?v=Vja1W8gV8dA.
4. Marker, "What If We Lost the Cheetah?"
5. Marker, "What If We Lost the Cheetah?"
6. Marker, "What If We Lost the Cheetah?"
7. Marker, "What If We Lost the Cheetah?"

Chapter Twenty-Four: Midori

1. Donna Perlmutter, "Midori: From Prodigy to Artist: Unlike Many *Wunderkinder*, the Japanese Violinist Has Made the Transition from Lollipops to Limousines," *Los Angeles Times*, April 8, 1990, https://www.latimes.com/archives/la-xpm-1990-04-08-ca-1631-story.html.
2. David Vernier, "Midori Receives Honorary Doctorate," Classics Today, https://www.classicstoday.com/midori-receives-honorary-doc torate/.
3. Midori, "Midori to Receive Kennedy Center Honor in Recognition of Lifetime Artistic Achievement," January 14, 2021, https://www.midori-violin.com/news/midori-to-receive-kennedy-center-hon or-in-recognition-of-lifetime-artistic-achievements/.

Chapter Twenty-Five: Julia Parsons

1. All quotes in this chapter from Julia Parsons, telephone conversation with the author, November 18, 2022.

Chapter Twenty-Six: Nancy Pelosi

1. Nancy Pelosi, telephone conversation with the author, September 8, 2020.

2. Pelosi, telephone conversation with the author.

3. Pelosi, telephone conversation with the author.

4. Nancy Pelosi and Amy Hill Hearth, *Know Your Power: A Message to America's Daughters* (New York: Anchor, 2009), 12.

5. Nancy Pelosi, Facebook post, January 20, 2011, https://www.facebook.com/NancyPelosi/photos/50-years-ago-today-i-was-a-young-trinity-college-student-standing-outside-in-the/10150134012599384/.

6. Pelosi, telephone conversation with the author.

Chapter Twenty-Seven: Kaitlin Roig-DeBellis

1. All quotes in this chapter from Kaitlin Roig-DeBellis, email message to the author, April 7, 2023.

Chapter Twenty-Eight: Buffy Sainte-Marie

1. Buffy Sainte-Marie, email message to the author, October 7, 2022.

2. Sainte-Marie, email message to the author.

3. "Buffy Sainte-Marie on Breastfeeding on Sesame Street in 1977," Yahoo Life, December 8, 2022, https://www.youtube.com/watch?v=OzWxY-Yaf8U.

4. "Buffy Sainte-Marie on Breastfeeding on Sesame Street in 1977."

5. Buffy Sainte-Marie, "Hey Little Rockabye—A Lullaby for Pet Adoption' Available Now," May 12, 2020, http://buffysainte-marie.com/?p=2644.

Chapter Twenty-Nine: Sheryl Sandberg

1. "Sheryl Sandberg, Barnard College Commencement 2011," Barnard College, May 17, 2011, https://www.youtube.com/watch?v=AdvXCKFNqTY.

2. Sheryl Sandberg, "Why We Have Too Few Women Leaders," TEDWomen, 2010, https://www.ted.com/talks/sheryl_sandberg_why_we_have_too_few_women_leaders.

3. Sandberg, "Why We Have Too Few Women Leaders."

4. "*Lean In* Discussion Guide," Lean In, March 2013, https://cdn-static.leanin.org/wp-content/themes/leanin/ui/resources/Lean_In_Discussion_Guide_All_Audiences.pdf?77f96d.

5. "Slow Down and Feel Your Feelings: Lean into the Suck," Option B, https://optionb.org/supporting-self/feel-your-feelings-lean-into-the-suck.

Chapter Thirty: Dr. Maya Shankar

1. All quotes in this chapter from "Google's Maya Shankar Delivers Keynote at Velocity 2019, UCLA Anderson's Women's Summit," UCLA Anderson, February 20, 2019, https://www.youtube.com/watch?v=h9y tufBRw4o&t=1341s.

Chapter Thirty-One: Lateefah Simon

1. "O's First-Ever Power List," *O, The Oprah Magazine*, September 2009, https://www.oprah.com/money/power-women-o-the-oprah -magazines-power-list/all.

2. Carolyn Jones, "Lateefah Simon: Youth Advocate Nominated as Visionary of the Year," *San Francisco Chronicle*, January 5, 2015, https://www.sfgate.com/visionsf/article/Lateefah-Simon-Youth-advo cate-nominated-as-5993578.php.

3. "New Mexico State Auditor and Executive Director of Lawyers' Committee for Civil Rights Honored by Caroline Kennedy as Recipients of 2010 John F. Kennedy New Frontier Awards," John F. Kennedy Presidential Library and Museum, December 1, 2010, https://www .jfklibrary.org/about-us/news-and-press/press-releases/new-mexico -state-auditor-and-executive-director-of-lawyers-committee-for-civil -rights-honored.

4. "Mills College 2017 Commencement—Lateefah Simon '17," Mills College at Northeastern, May 22, 2017, https://www.youtube.com /watch?v=dXaDyu46MhM.

5. "Lateefah Simon, TEDxOakland," TEDx, December 20, 2017, https://www.youtube.com/watch?v=0T9jQBVThts.

Chapter Thirty-Two: Erna Solberg

1. "After Softening, 'Iron Erna' Solberg Set to Become Norway's PM," Reuters, September 10, 2013, https://web.archive.org /web/20130911091254/http://www.dnaindia.com/world/1886754 /report-after-softening-iron-erna-solberg-set-to-become-norway-s-pm.

2. "After Softening, 'Iron Erna' Solberg Set to Become Norway's PM."

3. Erna Solberg, "How Can Investing in Women and Girls Accelerate Global Development beyond 2015?" Speech to World Economic Forum in Davos, Switzerland, January 24, 2015, https://awpc.cattcenter .iastate.edu/2017/03/09/how-can-investing-in-women-and-girls-accel erate-global-development-beyond-2015-jan-24-2015/.

4. Solberg, "How Can Investing in Women and Girls Accelerate Global Development beyond 2015?"

5. Solberg, "How Can Investing in Women and Girls Accelerate Global Development beyond 2015?"

6. Solberg, "How Can Investing in Women and Girls Accelerate Global Development beyond 2015?"

7. GPE Secretariat, "15 Women Leading the Way for Girls' Education." GPE, March 8, 2015, https://www.globalpartnership.org/blog/15-women-leading-way-girls-education.

8. GPE Secretariat, "15 Women Leading the Way for Girls' Education."

9. Garrett Walker, "Scandinavian Stability for a World in Flux: A Conversation with Norwegian Prime Minister Erna Solberg," *Harvard International Review*, June 7, 2020, https://hir.harvard.edu/scandinavian-stability-for-a-world-in-flux/.

10. Walker, "Scandinavian Stability for a World in Flux."

Chapter Thirty-Three: Dr. Sara Seager

1. Sara Seager, email message to the author, March 11, 2023.

2. Seager, email message to the author.

3. Seager, email message to the author.

4. Seager, email message to the author.

5. Seager, email message to the author.

6. Seager, email message to the author.

7. Sara Seager, "A Real Search for Alien Life," TEDxCambridge 2013, https://www.youtube.com/watch?v=NnM4SaGc8R0.

8. Sara Seager, "The Search for Planets beyond Our Solar System," TED2015, https://www.ted.com/talks/sara_seager_the_search_for_planets_beyond_our_solar_system.

9. Seager, "The Search for Planets beyond Our Solar System."

10. Seager, "A Real Search for Alien Life."

11. Seager, email message to the author.

Chapter Thirty-Four: Kathrine Switzer

1. All quotes in this chapter from Kathrine Switzer, "The Girl Who Started It All," *Runner's World*, Match 26, 2007, https://www.runnersworld.com/runners-stories/a20801860/kathrine-switzer-runs-the-boston-marathon/.

CHAPTER THIRTY-FIVE: TINA WELLS

1. Tina Wells, "Elevation by Tina Wells," February 2, 2023, https://tinawells.com/2023/02/02/elevation-by-tina-wells/.

2. Wells, "Elevation."

3. Wells, "Elevation."

4. Chana Twiggs, "Entrepreneur and Author Tina Wells Shares 5 Ways to Achieve Work-Life Balance," *Ebony*, March 9, 2023, https://www.ebony.com/tina-wells-5-ways-life-balance/.

5. Tina Wells biography, https://tinawells.com/bio/.

6. "My Cart Is Full with Tina Wells and Mona Swain," *Black Beyond Measure*, May 28, 2023, https://www.youtube.com/watch?v=1iJjUFiAq20.

7. Tina Wells biography.

8. "Black History Month Featuring Tina Wells." Ally Shoes, January 30, 2023, https://www.ally.nyc/blogs/news/black-history-month-featuring-tina-wells.

9. Twiggs, "Entrepreneur and Author Tina Wells."

10. "My Cart Is Full with Tina Wells and Mona Swain."

INDEX

ABOUT THE AUTHOR

Elisa Boxer is an Emmy and Murrow award–winning journalist whose work has been featured in publications including the *New York Times* and *Fast Company*. She has taught journalism at the college level and has reported for newspapers, magazines, and TV stations. Elisa has a passion for telling stories about trailblazing women breaking social barriers and finding the courage to create change. She is the author of several nonfiction children's books, including *The Voice That Won the Vote: How One Woman's Words Made History*, *A Seat at the Table: The Nancy Pelosi Story*, *One Turtle's Last Straw: The Real-Life Rescue That Sparked a Sea Change*, *SPLASH!: Ethelda Bleibtrey Makes Waves of Change* (a Junior Library Guild Gold Standard Selection), *Covered in Color: Christo & Jeanne-Claude's Fabrics of Freedom* (called "compelling from cover to cover" in a *Kirkus* starred review), and *Hidden Hope: How a Toy and a Hero Saved Lives During the Holocaust* (a Junior Library Guild Gold Standard Selection that received three starred reviews and was called "important" and "inspiring" in a *School Library Journal* starred review). Elisa lives in Maine and has more books on the way. Visit her at https://www.elisaboxer.com/.

9.

the Auther was Born In 1970
She Has written many books
and Likes to.

From *The Kitten and the Puppy,* by Elisa Boxer (1976)